SANDRA CURRY KELLER

Your

Soul's

History

CONNECTS EVERYTHING

ISBN ebook: 978-0-578-26771-5
ISBN paperback: 978-0-578-26772-2

I dedicate this book to my father. The love we shared in our past lives and this present one outlives any possession of land, money, or gold. Love continues on with God's divine guidance teaching all of us love is eternal. Without love, there is no meaning. Jesus preached his love on earth to everyone.

CONTENTS

PREFACE

My life started on Cape Cod, Massachusetts, in 1953 and was at the crossroads of life and death prior to my fourth birthday. I had a rare kidney disorder and was transferred to Massachusetts Children's Hospital in Boston. Home would be in this hospital for a long eight months. I was experimental, as I was the first female to have this rare kidney surgery performed.

The Cape Cod Times wrote several articles on me, and my home-town donated a lot of money towards my hospital care. The picture showed me visiting with my pastor and my mother after I was released from the hospital. Another article told how I needed to return to the hospital as the first surgery was not successful. I underwent the second surgery, and that one was a winner. I no longer needed to wear a bag on my small leg to urinate in.

I praise God for assisting my doctors creating this new kidney procedure to save my life. At four years old, I made medical history. I had many complications with kidney infections and always needed to have my antibiotics close by. Yes, they fixed me like a broken doll, but I was never really the same again. Other factors came in with bacteria always in my system, and children never came into my life.

God saved me for a reason, and I am so thankful to be alive. This was my first big test in life as a young child, learning how precious life truly was! I know now why God saved me, and my life has taken on new meaning through spiritualism.

Throughout my young life, I gravitated to church. I remember walking as a young child to go to church so I would not miss singing in the choir. Everyone else in my family would be snuggled up in their warm beds, sleeping while I walked in the snow to church. Our church was only a mile away, and I did not want to disturb my family. My parents and brothers would go on special holidays, but I tried to go every week. My father told me at a later date he got up and watched me walking with my Bible under my arm and admired me for that.

In 1985, my father was diagnosed with cancer. I searched deep into my soul and asked God to give me the spiritual strength to find a church that would help me cope with his inevitable death. At that time, I did not have a church I was happy with, and I lived in California. My father left Cape Cod ten years prior to be closer with me. It was a shock for me that my father actually left Cape Cod, where he was planning to die. The great love we shared for each other won out with that huge move. I was thirty-one years old then and was guided to a Christian spiritualist church. I never knew anything about a spiritualist church before.

My neighbor's daughter-in-law told me about a gifted minister who gave spiritual readings and asked me if I would like to go with her for a reading. Little did I know at that time she would be the instrument guiding me to my new church. After my incredible reading with Rev. Mitchell, he walked me through his house and showed me his small chapel on the other side of his home. It was crystal clear I would attend his church, and my prayers were answered. I studied spiritualism at this small church for ten years.

My father asked me to promise him that I would continue to fight for our twenty-three-acre family land on Cape Cod where the history of our seafaring ancestors, "the Perry's," was embedded. I looked into his eyes and made that promise to him I would fight for this family land.

As my father's illness progressed, culminating finally in his death, my spiritual awareness helped me to gain comfort and an understanding of the other side. My spiritual journey had begun.

During my spiritual journey, I came to understand early on that I was not alone. There are spirit guides who led me in the right direction to make me aware of them. When I asked for their guidance, they spoke to me. I listened, but I didn't always believe what they told me. Yes, I was stubborn and fell down many times while they watched me struggle.

With time, I understood their guidance was imperative for me to acquire my rare gift of "automatic writing through spirit." After ten years of studying spiritualism, I reached levels of awareness that astounded me. Never again in my life would there be silence, as words flowed out like a raging river to tell me I am with God! Having Spirit flow through to encourage me on my spiritual quest was awesome.

In the beginning, small steps were taken along my spiritual path. I was so intrigued to acquire more knowledge of the truth regarding life after death and awareness. Our small church was intimate and accessible, answering my myriad of questions instantly. To seek truth was my goal and to learn more and more as I continued on with my life.

Through my new gift of automatic writing, I was one who loved to ask questions and decided to give my spiritual readings with my clients to ask their most important questions. I advised my clients to always ask their important question first for their reading and then their second and third questions. I would say a prayer for that individual and send their name into the ethers. I was a channel to the other side for them.

Throughout the years, I gave readings only to family and mainly friends of friends who were referred to me. At first, it would take energy out of me when I gave my first readings. With time, it became natural to work with the other side to speak through me. Most of the time, loved ones would come in to assist with answers for their important questions asked. I do not use any tool to assist me, such as tarot cards most readers depend upon. I utilize my gift of automatic writing on paper for my client to leave with, and I speak verbally during the session.

I kept my promise to my father and could not fight all the greed, evil, and injustice in my home-town on the Cape. My relatives and a developer were after the land, and after a lengthy eight-year litigation, it was time to move on.

"Your Soul's History," was born, and my writing could not stop to tell my true-life story. It actually felt good writing about my hardships with the great faith I carried within my soul. I felt tormented for several years.

An opportunity presented itself through a Cayce teacher named Peter Woodward. Peter held a group regression and I followed up with a private regression the following day. I learned of my past life as I was an Egyptian man living during Christ's life, and I was a news bearer spreading the gospel of Jesus. I was really reporting news during that time, and it turned out to be about what Jesus was preaching. You could say; I was at the right place and time, and on the flip side of the coin, I was at the wrong place and time as well.

My regression started in the Roman arena waiting in line to be killed for being a Christian lover. Reincarnation stepped in through this regression of the past for me to understand why my gift is so powerful and important. Finally, I have proof of this past life cemented in with the words of this Egyptian man on a CD. One door closes and another door opens for me with truth to heal my soul with answers to my past.

I knocked on that door that I was led to by spirit, and now I know it was my spirit guide; Karnak, who set me free with the truth. This past life was so important for me, and I had the connection all along within my soul and needed to be patient after going through hell to be able to rejoice at the very end.

Opening this door of enlightenment of my past is leading me to a second book I am writing now, and I realize my ending is just the beginning. Don't ever be afraid to seek the truth, and please open your door to a new journey you never knew existed. Seek, and ye shall find; I did.

CHAPTER 1

A NARROW & CHILLING ESCAPE

In the order of our universe, have you ever thought how do I fit in? Who am I? What has made me who I am today? As you move forward in life, we all make choices as we continue through our journey on earth.

We all have different activities here. There are levels of growth throughout the years. Certain areas of interest sneak into our awareness with delight or joy of that particular subject. You are drawn to writing, painting, singing or playing the piano. This is your comfort area of peace and you are happy to experience and embrace it.

So, what is life all about? We are born and we all die. This is something we have in common life and death. Each one of us is a different snowflake. No two are the same. We are all particles of God as he is our creator.

The answer is within our soul. Your soul is a continuous piece of thread that goes on and on from your beginning until the very end. Some of you may be aware or have knowledge of reincarnation. I learned about reincarnation as I got older and wanted to understand more about this subject.

Prior to my father's death I cried out to God to guide me to a church that would suit me. My prayer was answered as I was invited to attend a spiritualist church. I studied spiritual understanding, meditation and healing classes. I had an important family member of mine going to the other side and wanted to absorb as much knowledge as possible. To be able to understand more led me on a spiritual journey as I needed answers to many questions I had.

Writing my book "Your Soul's History," portions of which you are about to read now, gave me great anxiety with the ending. I was tormented for several years as I did not like the ending. It was not until I received a flyer in the mail from the Edgar Cayce group to attend a group regression. Fortunately, I was a member of A.R.E. and was excited to go and experience this private past life reading for 90 minutes.

The knowledge that I had about my past life could not give proof with words or a confirmation like this! Finally, I could move on as I had received many answers to be able to move forward in my present life. It was as if Spirit guided me to go and seek the knowledge to set me free and to validate what I had written. My spiritual journey continued and I am happy to give you this incredible past life regression word for word. To hear the words are more powerful than reading, due to the emotions involved.

This regression has brought forward an important piece of my soul's spiritual journey, with answers to guide me further today. With the understanding of reincarnation, this regression has told me I have experienced the most important past life ever! Not only do I know who I was in a past life, but it holds the key to why my faith is so strong today. If I was not traveling, I never would have met the Son of God preaching wherever he could. I became a Christian as an Egyptian man, and his teachings remain in my soul now. Anyone who experienced this spiritual time in history (as it unfolded) was blessed and touched by Jesus coming into their lives knowing the true meaning of love.

I was there to listen to our Master Jesus, speaking to the crowds who listened intently to his every word. His words were powerful; and filled the air with love and kindness, for his followers to breathe into their souls. I knew then and now that Jesus is the way and the light to bring us home to God.

In my past life, I was exiled from Rome barely escaping the arena with my life. It ended up I was to go back to Egypt to spread the news of Christ. In my present life I am compelled to spread the word by writing a spiritual book about Christ. This shows how my past and present life intertwine perfectly. Your Soul's History, was my guiding light from earth and heavenly father's eternal love in heaven.

On September 12th, 2015, I attended a full day workshop in San Diego healing the past, building the future. A Cayce teacher, Peter Woodbury, who is also a psychotherapist, hypnotherapist, past life regressionist, and Harvard University graduate gave a special group hypnotic regression. The Edgar Cayce, in Virginia Beach, is where his Association for Research and Enlightenment Headquarters is located.

This workshop I attended gave the process of hypnosis and past-life regression and how it can be used for healing and self-awareness even if you don't believe in reincarnation! Do you want a personal experience channeling your Higher Self for guidance, soul healing, and an awareness of your divine connection? Travel to the Akashic "Hall of Records" and glimpse the record of your own soul's journey. Tap into past lives that are having a major impact upon the present.

cial group of hypnotic regression brought me back to my past and with a special person I knew I loved long ago. I saw this woman waving to me from across this huge river. I knew her and felt she was important to me by the way she was waving with great anticipation. I needed to know who she was to me.

After Peter's workshop I scheduled a private regression with him the next day. Peter put me under hypnosis, and I was regressed back to Christ's time. I was given several confirmations of my past life during the time of Christ and feel this confirmation has cemented my past life with words from this regression. These words were recorded and I will write them down for you to read. After my regression, I told Peter he was the "real deal." I am glad I decided to set up a regression, as these words given were paramount.

Listening to my words with the emotion in my voice was chilling. To be able to make the big escape from being killed in the Roman arena and traveling safely back to Egypt was a miracle. Spirit came through (after my regression was given) to inform me I was picked up by a Roman Informant for being a Christian. It was easy for this Roman Informant to have me arrested, as I was an Egyptian man, not a Roman Citizen. I stood in line with other Christians, Roman thieves and murderers waiting to be killed in the arena.

This informant was someone I considered a friend, and he was paid in gold for reporting my crime of being a Christian. Another friend saw me in line to be killed and went to a higher ranked Roman official to help me. This man of high importance was a friend who waited for my news of Christ. We spent hours together as I shared what I learned during my travels. He was one who I sat down with, to have good food and wine with much laughter. My visit was in the best house in Rome, and I had servants waiting on me as if I were the Master of the house. Can you imagine the feeling as I approached his mansion after a long journey of gathering the most important news? I had several more clients of wealth who became my friends. I shared my knowledge and received their lavish comforts as well. My hard work traveling and collecting the news of Jesus of the Gospel at that time was overwhelming with joy, but ended with betrayal by a friend, now an enemy.

My friend of importance told the man in charge of the line at the arena there was a terrible mistake! "I know this man and you need to release him now." I was released and my friend gave me money. "Go home and don't ever come back to Rome, my friend." I left frantically and found my way back to my mule and was on my way home. So much work left behind I could no longer do. My life was spared for a reason.

I believe my journey was meant to be for me to go back with my people of Egypt to speak and teach Christ's words. The knowledge I acquired is in my soul and carries on with great honor to have met our Master Jesus Christ himself along my travels.

I was told to describe in words what I am experiencing during the regression. It took a while for the words to come out. So many words were given and then, after long pauses more words would flow. A story is told, and I had no idea what would come next.

Here it goes:

Cheering...many many people...arena of some sort...lots of noise...people chanting and big event...animals around underneath...people being dragged and thrown into this big area...big circle...horrifying for those in the center...and the others...spectators looking watching...a place you don't want to be if you're in the center of it all and everyone is watching

you watching…death is prevalent here…you can't escape it…
nowhere to go…nowhere to hide…SO CLOSE TO BEING
INSIDE THERE…it was a normal event for some…and others
just wanted to run…escape and hide…have to get away…have
to get away…can no longer be around here…outside leaving…
further and further away from all of it…must go home…I'm
on a long journey… this journey is very far far away…going
home…home where I'll be safe…and my journey will end
there. But I will be back with my own people, and I will share
what I have learned to help my people understand better and
I will share the knowledge of Jesus Christ our Lord and I
shall speak with everyone…everyone that I know and whoever
wants to hear the words of Christ. I will not be afraid. I will
speak the truth and be safe here. I left a lot of people behind…
people who became friends…friends turned into enemies…
others protected me…made me go along my way…had to exit
leave… leave what I became accustomed to…the good food…
the good wine…the good company…and the good money I
received…I had to give that all up…for my own safety…so I
go back…I go home…I really don't want to go home not right
now…not yet…not when things are so crucial…but I must
go…I can no longer stay…so I will go…on my journey to
another way of life…to teach and belong with my own people…
share my experiences and hopefully provide what they need…
as I have learned across my many travels…I will go home…
but I will speak loud…I will be so happy to be able to share
my news my great news for all of us. To be able to know and
experience what is happening now, what is going on. I am home
and I am safe. I thank my friends who helped me. There is a
big river…there is this woman on the other side of this river…
she waves to me…she seems to be very happy to see me…I
think she has been waiting for me for a long time…I need

to cross this river to get to her…I am working on getting to cross the river to be with her again. She has been so patient… waiting waiting waiting…it has been 3 years, a little over 3 years since I have seen her. We are together again…I tell her of my journeys… many many journeys…while I was gone… now she says she is so happy I will not make any more…not so far away…not so long in time…she has great comfort of me being home, safe, alive…traveling at a distance now will be no more long distance… close to home…roads shorter to where I'll be going where I'll be speaking in Egypt… traveling is too dangerous…so my wife is so happy very happy she has me now…close to home.

In the end, I received through this regression the knowledge of who I once was again. I knew I had walked with Christ. Being able to verify with other people through their special gifts brings great comfort to me. This past life tells me why my faith is so strong. I was there to listen to our Master, Jesus, speaking to the crowds who listened with great intensity to his every word. His words were powerful, filled with so much love and kindness. To be living during that precious time was an amazing event in our spiritual history. The knowledge given by Jesus has left a mark on my soul that carries through each incarnation giving immeasurable joy to not fear death. I know Jesus is the way and the light to bring us home to God.

On March 4, 2018 Peter Woodbury came to San Diego and held a class for Soul Lessons and Soul Patterns. I requested a private past life regression with him to seek more information during Christ's time. I asked him to take me back as the Egyptian man I was to gather more information during this time period.

I held a lot of anticipation of what I would receive during this time of spiritual history. Information was given to me as Peter told me I would receive more from this past life, as the door was there and to open it any time. This is what happened with my second regression.

Peter put me under hypnosis and this regression was completely different. It took me some time to figure it all out after I left. I needed to process the whole regression. There were no words given at all this time. A story of words flowed on my last regression giving great details starting in the Roman arena during Christ's time. I could not speak with words as my journey started leaving my home land of Egypt to travel to far away countries.

A vision was given of me kissing and hugging a woman goodbye. As I rode my mule, I kept looking back at her with a large smile and continued to wave until I no longer saw her. I was riding through the desert for days and days. My mouth was covered with a large piece of cloth as I rode, as the wind and sand blew on me.

No words could come out when I was under hypnosis due to the cloth across my mouth. I tried to speak and it was mumbled and I realized later why I could not speak.

As I continued to ride on my mule I would jump up in the chair as if I was riding over an area in the desert that had a bump. Throughout this regression I jumped up in my chair several times and continued to ride on my mule. There was no end riding across the desert, especially when you only have 90-minute duration of time for your regression.

Now I know I left my wife and traveled to lands far away to share news that would be the greatest news of all time. This woman who waved to me in the group regression was so important to me that her appearance came in each regression. She was my Egyptian wife I left and came home to over 3 years later.

The great love I held for this woman was a mystery and there is more to come with her as she is a past-life connection in my present. This story needs to be told, but from over two thousand years ago continues on in a present life today. More will be revealed about her as the past and the present is all out of great love!

Peter told me sometimes people do not talk during their regression. They just relax and say they received peace and enjoyed it. Everyone is different and experience what they need. Then other people chatter away and tell a story.

I felt it was important for me to go back to leaving Egypt to show this woman for a reason. The important piece of mystery is who she ended up being in my present life.

This was important for me, but I did not realize it until several years later. I was really blown away when I found out who she was to me and should have known all along! In my soul I knew, but needed to bring this information to the present.

A SPIRITUAL AWAKENING

After reading my past life regression, I am sure each and every one of you wonders what was your past life regression? Where were you in time that the past life you experienced was etched in your soul? We all have one that remains within and if you seek the knowledge, you will receive the answer. Knock and the door shall open.

For myself, I always knew who I was in the past, but to prove it with words cemented in was exactly what I needed. It was a confirmation given to me at just the right time. At times you question yourself and without being guided you lose your way. It is that great faith you need and you will receive it when you allow spirit to come in. To understand all of it has almost taken me a life time to discover the complete story.

As a young child I was always captivated with movies during Christ's time with the Romans riding their chariots. Ben Hur is one of my favorite movies as I felt like I was right there. The arena would give me chills, as I could relate to those people being thrown in and killed. There was a fixation for me to watch and not realizing at that time I experienced that past life.

In my home today on my hutch is a collection of Egyptian plates. Isis and Osiris are on the top shelf along with my three wise men in the middle. For my birthday my girlfriend Anita sent me these two famous pieces in statue form of Isis and Osiris. She had a collection of Egyptian items and found out I had one as well. I welcomed my new treasures, and I was happy to add them to my huge Egyptian collection. My friends Jacquie and Sue have showered me with their unique Egyptian trinkets as well. This past life in Egypt and Rome was intense. I bought a huge painting of Rome showing the villas, the sailboats in the ocean and all the beautiful flowers. Still in my soul today.

Isis was the goddess who encapsulated the virtues of the archetypal Egyptian wife and mother. Isis was the sister wife to Osiris and mother to Horus. Osiris was one of the most important deities of ancient Egypt. Osiris is associated with death, resurrection, and fertility. He is usually depicted as a mummy whose hands project through his wrappings to hold the Royal Insignia, the Crook, and the Flail.

My second shelf consists of a large Egyptian perfume bottle with smaller ones surrounding it. There are large camels with their baby camels on each side of the parents. On the other side, I have an art piece called Ramose and Wife. I was drawn to this Egyptian man and woman at the Luxor in Las Vegas during my honeymoon. Huge Egyptian tiles of art were hanging on all their walls. Out of all the beautiful art pieces, I gravitated to the Egyptian man and woman. I knew in my soul I had to buy it! This was my honeymoon gift to myself.

The story went that this Egyptian man Ramose loved this one Egyptian woman and had only her for his wife. In those days he could have had many wives, but chose one wife to adore and love. Little did I know the importance of this art piece until a much later time. My third shelf consists of marble pyramid, sphinx, Pharaoh and other marble gems.

My father and brother Jeoffrey were Merchant Marines and traveled to Egypt at different times. My father worked on the Woods Hole Oceanographic and they traveled with scientists in 1965 to the Red Sea and visited Egypt. He bought a large plaque of Queen Nefertiti which consisted of bronze copper and gold leaf. It tells the whole story of her life. He also brought back many other Egyptian items hung in the rest of my house.

My brother Jeoffrey visited Egypt in 1975 when he was in the Navy. He was there when President Saddat worked with us and reopened the Suez Canal. There is a beautiful picture of the three pyramids with the sphinx in front that he brought home. Yes, I acquired it and hung it on the side of my hutch. Jeoffrey also gave me large Egyptian papyrus pictures and hung their beauty throughout my house. The world's first paper was Papyrus. It is made from thin slices of the stalk of the papyrus plants, which grow in the Nile River of Egypt.

The most important piece is my large picture of Jesus of Nazareth on the right side of my hutch. I had the history of my past life on my hutch telling me who I was for years. As an Egyptian man, finding Christianity and being almost killed in the arena was a rare event. It all came together like a large puzzle that takes time to enter each piece just right.

In February 2019 it all came together, as I found out who this woman was who waved at me across this huge river. The huge river turned out to be the Nile in Egypt. I attended a group regression with Peter Woodbury in 2015. This information was given to me after I figured out who this important past life woman was!

At first, I did not connect the dots of my past life of who this Egyptian wife was in my present life. I thought maybe this woman was my mother in this past life. That is why I explored more and followed up with an appointment with Peter for a private regression.

You need to realize that we all need to experience being a man or a woman and I was blind-sided with thinking the woman in the past, was also a woman in my present life. I was totally wrong, as I discovered my Egyptian wife during Christ's time ended up being a man in my present life. The love connection is there, but gender and relationship roles change. I am a woman and a daughter in this present incarnation.

I was lying in bed thinking, "Who was this important Egyptian woman who was my wife?" This journey of going back over two thousand years told a story of my most important past life ever! I was the Egyptian man who traveled and left my wife to become a news bearer during a crucial time of spiritual history being made.

During my regression, Peter told me more information would come to me later. The door would always be open. I always had questions and felt stupid; because I did not know who this woman was at the beginning. How could I have not known?

In January 2019, my past and present had a turn of events with my book "Your Soul's History." My ending chapter became my beginning chapter. Two significant times of my life included greed, evil, and injustice. Two stories became one and finally connected history as the key element. Without history, who are we? This pertains to your soul as well. Your past life is like a movie; when you go back in time to that precious moment connecting who you truly are today. My movie of great importance; begins during the greatest story ever told about the spiritual history of Jesus. That past life is hard to disconnect or shake out of your soul when it is there forever, like being branded!

In all reality, my past life relates to the present and intertwines perfectly to bring the truth of reincarnation and how important it is to be able to move forward in your present.

I am a prime candidate as the mystery finally came out about who my past life wife was in Egypt.

My past life wife of Egypt was my father in my present life. My book "Your Soul's History," was written out of great love promising my father to continue his fight to save family land on Cape Cod. Yes, it took me a long time to figure that out when it should have been a given. I was told by past readers that my father and I spent four different lifetimes together. One of them was where we were married in a past life. I even had a flash back one time of kissing my father on the cheek and it felt like we shared a closer relationship. Well, we did, and it was stunning! You know you are close with someone, and we don't have all the answers because we leave that information on the other side. My mother told me that my father had morning sickness for her when she was carrying me. Sometimes, the husband has morning sickness instead of the wife. I found that information interesting.

I meditated the next morning; after I figured out it was my father all along with this past life of great love. I asked, "Who was my Egyptian wife?" The answer I received was this: Who do you think? Of course, it was me. I drove across country to be close to you. Not your brothers, you! You mentioned you felt me coming. For a whole week, I felt my father so strong and there he was on my doorstep!

We spent several lives together. You are my angel, and we will be connected again out of the great love we have. You did not die as a young child. You had a reason to live.

You always took care of me. You were there until the end of my life and gave all your love the last two years and before

I died. You kept in touch with me throughout the years and spent time caring for whatever I needed. I thank you for being with me. You broke off your engagement and quit your full-time job for me. That was great love!

The important element of discovering your past life is for you to know what truly happened to you during that time period. Your life will take on a new meaning of who you were and where you have been. You knocked on that door and it opened with the truth, giving you answers to validate what you thought you experienced. This is a gift from God to guide you and know there is much more to come in your next life.

It has taken many years for me to realize the focus of my book is to share the truth about spiritualism and reincarnation. I feel privileged to be able to tap into my past and write about it. From one day to the next, you never know everything, and I will never give up on my questions that I constantly ask about our universe.

We continue on due to our soul that never dies. Your energy that leaves your body is your soul going to another dimension. One human body suit is rented to us one life time after another. You do not have a body when you go to the other side, but you always keep your soul wherever you are. During your next spiritual lesson, you may connect with others who assist you with love, or have hurt you in the past. You need to know this happens and you eventually go home to God. Depending upon your travels of being good or bad is where you end up on the other side. Just know it is all good where there is nothing but God surrounding you with his love.

I journeyed back to the past of over two thousand years ago riding my mule across the sand dunes of Egypt and will take you to the dunes on Cape Cod in my present life. Behind me and in my present life I experienced greed, evil and injustice at different times. People from long ago came back into my life for a reason for me to understand the past. The past is who I was and what happened to me to bring me to a higher spiritual understanding of all of it. I believe I needed to experience the past and have my father assist me to know there is a higher purpose in life. The love for my father with this promise, I gave took me back when my life was spared. There is a reason for everything.

Leaving Egypt on a mule to travel across the desert to be a news bearer was daring and took courage. Never realizing how this journey would change my whole life, while others would learn about Christianity through me. I lived and many other people died, not being able to talk about our Lord Jesus Christ.

My mystery of the past and present connected the power of great love. This love never dies and comes back over and over again. The ending to my book has taken on a whole new meaning where I am released of the torment, I carried for too many years. I truly know now with my encounter with Jesus that LOVE is all that matters. The family land I promised to fight for was not that important after all. It was who I was in the past and now I can share how good always shines through and blows evil away. I live today, although I almost died as a young child and almost died in the Roman arena to be a messenger.

When you lose that person, you have known many lifetimes the love scale goes higher and higher. I remember when I was walking after losing my father I would almost choke thinking in my mind of his loss. For about a week or so my head felt like I had 50 bricks on top as if my brain would explode! With time the heaviness of the bricks was released from my head. Grief is a process you can't escape. The greater the love, the higher the pain is.

In 2004 I bought property in the desert thinking my husband Fred and I might need to retire somewhere else. I bought a one-acre parcel in Pahrump, Nevada which is high desert. I understand now why I bought this property, because of my past connection with the desert. I always carry plenty of water in my car when I visit the desert, as you can never have enough water.

I still have my desert property in Nevada and my brother Jeoffrey lives there now. There are about 30 trees and he is the gardener and the trees are beautiful with Mount Charleston surrounding Pahrump Valley. The Las Vegas people drive up the huge mountain to go skiing. Plenty of water is derived from Mount Charleston, as cattle used this area many years ago for their old watering hole. Pahrump is about two hours away from Death Valley. I installed a 200 foot well on my property. There were trees on the property when I bought it and my acre was split from the adjoining acre water line. In the past as in the present water still keeps all of us alive. Our source of water is great for our farmers, cattle and all life. The Nile River was the source for Egypt and even went all the way to Africa with water to sustain life!

As we leave the past behind into the present, the greed, evil and injustice is there. Over two thousand years in time where people remain the same. We come back and some people grow spiritually, while others stay as they were with little spiritual growth. We all have our own free will to choose our path.

You have met them again in the present and know you don't want to deal with them in any capacity. You were enemies in the past and need to do business in the present. It is difficult because you can't run away from it, so you continue and ask God for guidance. Wisdom is given when asked and you need to be patient. There is a lesson here for you. What is this lesson you must endure?

For myself, I now have peace in my mind as I know exactly what to do next. I will continue to write and will be guided with my faith. I received the answers from long ago and will be a messenger for you in my upcoming book "*Your Soul's History,*" as I was in my past life.

CHAPTER 3

THE GREATEST STORY EVER TOLD

The story of Jesus is the greatest story ever told. For over 2,000 years, Jesus Christ has touched billions of people around the globe. Understanding Western history tells us the story of Jesus and his great love for all humanity. Yes, the story of Jesus Christ is well known and documented. Without this man, Jesus, the world would not understand the meaning of true love.

We all know of the life of Jesus from the Bible and movies. The reason why, after 2,000 years, he is still within our hearts and souls is because he was a simple man. He felt what we felt and faced what we all face today. We are all children of God: you could say particles of God. Jesus had a Chart as a messenger leaving us as the Son of God. Jesus showed humankind the way to love each other and taught the simplicity of spiritualism. "Seek and you shall find" and "Knock and it shall be opened to you." Therefore, Christianity was introduced through Jesus. We may not all be on the same page regarding all the facts about Jesus. We have been taught, through whatever religion we were brought up with, certain rituals of our church. The Christian religion holds baptism as a ritual with water on one's head or immersed in water. Jesus was baptized by John the Baptist on the banks of the River Jordan. The baptism was for people to turn away from their sins and turn to God.

The Roman Catholic Church usually baptizes infants to free them from the original sin they were born with. It is their way to welcome them into the Catholic Church. The Baptist Church baptizes in the name of the Trinity the Father, the Son and the Holy Spirit. However, they do not believe that baptism is necessary for salvation; rather, it is an act of Christian obedience.

They use the three most common practices with sprinkling water on a person's forehead, pouring water over the head or immersing completely under the water. Most churches practice baptizing adults or believers by complete immersion.

I experienced my baptism at eleven years old, like Jesus by complete immersion, and mine was in a lake. It was a spiritual experience of accepting Christ into my life forever. After my baptism, I felt embraced with love and spiritually connected. As an infant, the baptism would hold no memory or substance of faith. Christians believe that once you believe and have faith in Christ, you are born again.

There was no other man like Jesus on earth. He was different and stood out like a neon light of gentleness and love. He preached so everyone could understand what he meant. They were simple words for all who wanted to listen. There were many parables given to provide spiritual lessons from Jesus. He was like a magnet who drew you in to hear more of his sermons. You could never receive enough words of wisdom from him. No one knew how special Jesus was at that time in Galilee. As he preached more to the people, there was an admiration that grew for him. People wanted to hear more and sought him out about where he would preach next.

Jesus was charismatic and a great speaker who meant every word he spoke. His life was not easy, as he traveled miles and miles to do his work for his father. His mission on earth held great faith for him to heal the sick and have one miracle after another with God's blessings. Jesus performed twenty-six recorded miracles, and there could have been more we don't know about.

The Jews, his own people, rejected him and persecuted him, as he did not follow the Jewish religion to the letter of their law. Jesus spoke with all Jewish people, and they pushed him back to a cliff in anger against his words, which did not go along with their faith. It was the highest-ranking Jew who put Jesus' life in jeopardy. They did not believe Jesus was the coming Messiah written from the Bible. There was great jealousy against Jesus, as the Jews and the Romans were losing control of their own people. Many Romans were intrigued by this man preaching to the masses. Jesus had a very strong following of his own. You could say he was like a rockstar, except you didn't have to give him any money.

If you were there during that time of spiritual history, you would have felt the greatest love ever. In his heart, Jesus held no hate, only pure love that flowed out like no other man on earth. He was the true Son of God, who came to teach us how important love is. Jesus was the only prophet to give healings with a simple touch of his hands. Many miracles were given as well to feed people and turn water into wine and much more. He even raised people from the dead! Jesus radiated love to everyone he met throughout his life, as teaching humankind was his mission.

Jesus was different from the beginning of his life, as a baby and Joseph. The only room available was with the animals, and Jesus was laid in a crib made from a horse trough. Three Wise Men from the East traveled a long distance to visit with baby Jesus. Three gifts were given with a spiritual meaning. Gold was a symbol of royalty, as Jesus was "King of the Jews;" frankincense, which represented the baby's holy nature as the Son of God; and myrrh to signify Jesus's mortality.

The Wise Men were Magi which meant they followed astrology. These Wise Men from the East followed the Star of Bethlehem and they say this star could have been a supernova. A supernova is a star that suddenly increases greatly in brightness because of a catastrophic explosion that ejects most of its mass. This star may reach a maximum intrinsic luminosity one billion times that of the sun. After the birth of Jesus, the Wise Men found baby Jesus to welcome him into the world. There has been controversy with the timing of this monumental meeting.

When Jesus was twelve years old, he went to Jerusalem on a pilgrimage with his parents, relatives and friends. During that time, the age of adulthood was twelve years old. This pilgrimage was called Passover, and this particular year, Jesus was allowed to go. The large group of family and friends went home without Jesus. Mary and Joseph went back to Jerusalem and found Jesus three days later. Jesus was fascinated with the temple and walked in like he belonged there. There was a topic of high intensity of religion and knowledge the rabbi and Jesus shared. It was amazing that such a young boy would be able to converse with a Jewish rabbi about God. Mary and Joseph realized Jesus was special, to find their son in the temple instead of other places of interest for their son to escape to.

Now, you need to realize that all things written about Jesus were not accurate. We have gathered information from various sources that give validation to stories that were made up.

Fabricating certain events written in the Bible happened quite a bit. Christ was of royal lineage and was portrayed as poor, when in reality, he was wealthy. Therefore, going into the temple was not a problem for Jesus to speak and teach with the Jewish rabbi. Jesus had a bloodline that included King Solomon and King David.

At twelve years old, if Jesus was just as wise as the rabbi in the temple, don't you think Jesus needed to study elsewhere for the wisdom they could not provide? The Jewish religion would not be what Jesus would settle for. Their laws were strict, and any variation made would not be tolerated by them.

When Mary and Joseph found Jesus in the temple, he told them, "I must be about my father's business." They did not understand, but Christ knew at that time what his purpose would be. These were the theologians of the Sanhedrin (lawmakers of Israel), and they listened to Jesus teach them because of his royal blood. Any other young boy would have been tossed out on their ear. This incident never would have come into being, unless this was not a true fact.

In his mid-teens, Jesus wanted to leave home and travel to explore other countries and their religions. There was a thirst for more spiritual knowledge that Jesus would not be able to find in his homeland in Nazareth. This travel of his would be necessary for Jesus to put together his religious beliefs. At a later date, the philosophies from other countries would be implemented in the creation of Christianity throughout the world.

The years when Jesus traveled were called the unknown, missing or the lost years. The story of Jesus being cruel to leave his family after the father's death was not true. Joseph died and left Mary with enough money, most likely for the rest of her life. Jesus was not, cruel in leaving his mother, as the family was well cared for. To leave home around twelve or thirteen years old to travel far away for many years without any money was not logical. Jesus knew he needed to leave to seek the knowledge necessary for his spiritual growth. Jesus was free to travel now and was away from the strict teachings of the Sanhedrin rabbis. His spiritual path was unfolding for him to seek the truth and wisdom he so desired.

These missing years would end up being some of the happiest times for him to experience. It must have been scary, to leave home that young, but it was exciting to go explore other countries and their religions.

Everyone loves a mystery, and the Bible did not share this time while Jesus traveled. You need to remember this was during a time of great change brewing. There are several versions of stories about what happened to Jesus in his teens and up to around thirty years old. There were no written records of this time of this walkabout Jesus took. Here is the most famous man in the world who left for many years and came back with his own philosophies. Where did Jesus get his knowledge from, and where did he get his ethics? The world would never be the same after Christianity is introduced from the Son of God. You could say this missing chapter was not meant to be read. This is a sacred chapter for Jesus only! Or is it?

One version was Jesus studied in Turkey, where he met scholars, merchants, and theologians and was introduced to beliefs in Gnosticism. This area was known as Constantinople and today is Istanbul. Jesus was a seeker of knowledge and wisdom and learned the philosophies during his travels. Even as a young man, Jesus made and left an impression on the individuals and crowds he encountered.

Another version is Jesus studied in Persia, known as Iran, and went eastward through Afghanistan and eventually into ancient India. Jesus studied Buddhism in India for many years and continued to Kashmir and Tibet. There he studied with teachers and masters and avidly learned from them. Jesus became a Yogi and learned of reincarnation.

Others say he did not travel and worked as a carpenter and studied in Nazareth for eighteen years. Then as Jesus became older, he left India and traveled to Egypt. Some say while Jesus was there, he studied the ancient Egyptian and Persian mysteries and more Gnostic teachings. After that, he then traveled to Qumran and lived and studied with the Essenes. The Essenes were private people and accepted Jesus as an Essene. Their community would not allow just anyone in.

John the Baptist was an Essence, and Jesus was his cousin, but at the time John baptized Jesus, he did not know Jesus was his cousin. They had not seen each other for many years until the time of the baptism of Jesus. The last time John saw Jesus is when he was a small boy. When John baptized Jesus, he saw the Spirit descending from heaven like a dove, and it rested upon him. John had no idea that Jesus was the actual Messiah the other prophets had foretold was coming.

Qumran is a region located in the West Bank, near the northern edge of the Dead Sea. The Dead Sea Scrolls were found in this region in 1947 and helped us understand the Jewish world in which Jesus lived. These scrolls were found in clay jars in the caves. The Dead Sea Scrolls are a priceless link to the Bible's past and have been attributed to the Essenes.

In 1947, in Nag Hammadi Upper Egypt, the Gnostics got their revenge with a great discovery of a lost gospel. There were thirteen leather-bound volumes discovered by Egyptian farmers. This lost gospel was a collection of Gnostic biblical texts that were excluded from the Bible. Comprising, among others, the gospel of Thomas, Peter, Mark, Judas and Mary, these writings depict a Christianity connected with a more human Jesus, perhaps more like the historical Nazarene rabbi of the first century.

This alleged lost gospel reveals Jesus was married to Mary Magdalene and had several children together. The mystery woman, Mary Magdalene, was the key witness to the cross, risking her own life to remain while the disciples fled for their lives. Mary was the messenger who told the apostles she saw Jesus' resurrection. After the resurrection, Mary is forgotten. To others, Mary Magdalene was the true Holy Grail. Mary Magdalene was a Canaanite priestess who became the revered center of a Church of the Gentiles movement based on his teachings.

Christian texts depicted Mary Magdalene as not just a mere follower, but Jesus's trusted companion, which some interpreted to mean his wife. For three hundred years during the time of Christ, the Jews would marry; even when they were a rabbi, marriage was a normal act. All the priests and popes were also married until the church changed the rules. Under the Jewish law, it was stated in the First Commandment to be fruitful and multiply. Jesus was not a celibate and unmarried man, as portrayed in the Roman Catholic Orthodox or in King James Version of the Bible.

This would make sense, as Mary Magdalene held appearances being close to Jesus. Mary was at the cross, bathing Jesus only as a wife would do and announcing the stone had rolled away from the tomb of Jesus. All the other disciples were not there like Mary Magdalene was. The other disciples ran in fear of being crucified themselves. Mary stood strong as only a loving wife would do.

Mary Magdalene was a missionary and preached to the people of her city in Greek and Aramaic. She also gave baptisms. She came from Magdala, a village on the western shore of the Sea of Galilee that was primarily known as a fishing town. There were many women named Mary during those days, and Mary the prostitute was a different Mary, not Mary of Magdala.

In 1969, Pope Gregory declared Mary Magdala was not a harlot. Why, after all this time, did the church decide to tell the truth? Did the holy church have something to hide? It is strange that Mary did not hold any status of wife, mother or daughter anywhere. She was called Mary of Magdala. The city she came from was Magdala. I do believe the church hated her, and they could not continue to label her a harlot any longer. New evidence from the Dead Sea Scrolls released her of this horrible crime of never being a harlot. Mary was a spiritual person Jesus fell in love with.

The disciples were jealous of Mary Magdalene due to the high-interest Jesus displayed toward her. Jesus would kiss her on the lips and showed signs of much greater love toward Mary. It would make sense, Jesus being closer, as Mary was his wife and they shared children. Therefore, she was excluded from the Bible, as there was jealousy involved, and the church would not give a woman recognition of any kind in those days. I believe Mary Magdala was the first Christian woman! Mary waited for Jesus to return from his many years of traveling and studying religion to marry him. Some say they knew each other as children and wrote letters to each other during those missing years of Jesus. They both shared preaching the Word of God and joined in holy matrimony, and united in Spirit.

Remember, the wedding at Cana where Jesus turned water into wine? Usually, the groom of a Jewish marriage, is responsible for having enough wine for all of his guests. Mary, the mother of Jesus, asked her son to acquire more wine during the wedding reception at Cana. It was highly embarrassing for a Jewish wedding to run out of wine, and it was the groom's duty to provide the wine. Jesus most likely was the groom and used his gift as a miracle to provide more wine for his guests. I think Mary, the mother, might have known Jesus could do this miracle. Mary knew Jesus could take a bad situation and make it right and even make it better than anyone could have imagined!

When the master of the feast tasted the water now become wine, and did not know where it came from (though the servants who had drawn the water knew), the master of the feast called the bridegroom and said to him, "Everyone serves the good wine first, and when people have drunk freely, then the poor wine. But you have kept the good wine until now." (John 2:9-10)

In 2006, The DaVinci Code movie was introduced to us with Tom Hanks and Audrey Tautou. This movie revealed codes in Leonard DaVinci's famous painting "The Last Supper." This movie received mixed reviews.

Then, in November 2014 filmmaker Simcha Jacobovici created "The Lost Gospel." In the British Library, there was a 6th--century manuscript found in plain sight. This was a 1500-year-old manuscript that would have been snuffed out by the church. This movie gives information about Mary Magdalene and Jesus being married and having children together.

You need to remember it took forty years or more after Jesus died before anything was written about him. There were fifty gospels written, and only four got entered into the Bible. There was a great debate of what would be written into the Bible and what would be eliminated by the church. During that time, many inconsistencies occurred.

The Pauline letters were entered in at the Council of Nicaea 325 A.D., when the Roman emperor Constantine made Pauline Christianity the state religion of Rome, and it became the

Roman Catholic Church. All other versions of Christianity that had survived for some 300 years were burned, the people sometimes along with them. The Pauline Christians could delete or add the gospels they chose for the Bible. Apostle Paul did not write the letters, but they were attributed to him within the letters themselves.

With all the history of the Roman Catholic Church and all the power they possessed throughout the years, I am inclined to think and feel there was a definite cover-up. Did the church keep a secret or secrets? We may never know the extent of all of it, to acquire the power they ended up with remains within the church. Or does it?

The story of Joseph of Arimathea is told in all four gospels. Joseph was a wealthy man who came from Arimathea in Judea. He was a good and righteous man who some say was a member of the Sanhedrin (the council) and a secret supporter of Jesus. Another source I found fascinating was that Joseph of Arimathea was a Decurion. A Decurion was a prestigious Roman title, often given to a prominent citizen. Joseph had connections with the mining industry that the Romans dealt with. His wealth came from the tin mines in England. During those missing years of Jesus, it has been said that Joseph took Jesus to England on his business trips. This would have been when Jesus got out in the world sailing with this wealthy uncle. If your father died when you were around twelve years old and your rich Uncle Joseph invited you to sail to England during his many business trips, I say that it would be a hard offer to refuse. As Jesus got older, he ventured out on his own to study in other areas.

If Jesus survived the cross, he might have made a safe refuge back to England. Jesus would not have been a stranger to England, as he sailed at a young age with his Uncle Joseph.

During this time of persecution would be the best time to leave with his family to be safe and far enough away. Joseph of Arimathea founded the church at Glastonbury, England. The story continues on there with more history.

According to Malcolm Bowden, the burial of criminal's bodies was the responsibility of relatives. If they were not claimed, they were consigned to be cast out as rubbish in an unmarked grave. Many who were killed on the cross stayed there until they rotted away. So, Joseph was not a member of the Sanhedrin but a prominent member of a Provincial Roman Senate or "advisory council," probably to Pilate himself. This would explain why Joseph could go directly to Pilate, who would know him well and that he was related to Jesus, so he released the body to him.

The rest of the story with the Great Uncle Joseph was that there was a secret plan to try to keep Jesus alive. Pilate assisted with special privileges provided to keep Jesus alive and to remain in his physical body. Uncle Joseph, Pilate, Judas and Mary Magdalene were in on this risky plan. Pilate had close guards to handle careful instructions to complete the survival of Jesus after the beatings and the suffering on the cross.

I would like to think that Jesus and Mary were married and had several children together.

The Lost Gospel claims evidence of it now with the Dead Sea Scrolls. If, in the end, Jesus somehow experienced the pain and suffering on the cross and lived, I would be eternally grateful to God and the people who assisted Jesus. I believe God did intervene through Pilate's wife having the dream about Jesus. In the dream, it was given that Jesus should not be harmed, and Pilate respected his wife's counsel.

Pilate tried many times to save Jesus as he felt Jesus was no threat. In the end, Pilate and Jesus knew the cross was inevitable. If Jesus lived after the cross, I don't feel any divinity would be taken away from him. Other prophets did not die and held their divinity as the good people they were. Think about whatever story or version you like, as Jesus was a Savior for all humankind and, in the end, teaching us about his eternal love.

The church made Jesus a martyr whether he wanted it or not. Jesus followed his chart, and his destiny was to teach the world a new religion called Christianity. Therefore, Jesus was not recognized until many years later for all the miracles he performed. I pray Jesus escaped with his family after all the hate he endured, especially by his own people!

If anyone could survive after the cruelty of being nailed to the cross, I sure would think God could intervene to save Jesus for all he did for humankind. Joseph of Arimathea had ships to sail away with the whole family as far as England. After the resurrection, there was never another word mentioned about Mary Magdalene. The mystery of Jesus and Mary continues.

Who Knows? There may be much more to find in the future, as the truth has a way of coming to the surface.

I was compelled to write this chapter about Jesus, and I learned so much while doing my own research. Once I started, I could not stop investigating, as I was intrigued to know more. My book, "*Your Soul's History,*" could not have been written without Jesus touching my very soul the way he did. I was blessed to meet this loving man Jesus, who changed our history through Christianity then and now.

CHAPTER 4

REINCARNATION AND REGRESSIONS

Some of you have never thought too much about rein-carnation. There are billions of people who do believe in reincarnation around the world. If you are one who has little knowledge of this subject, I would like to share my view with you.

I was one who was not brought up with the teachings of reincarnation, but as a young child, I was drawn to certain areas in other countries. These interests I held within and had great fascination and explored more as I became an adult.

Reincarnation is possibly the oldest and most widely held spiritual belief known to humankind. It is a belief held by ancient religions, but by current ones as well. There are people not just in India or other exotic countries, but probably living right next to you.

Most Christians are taught that you go to heaven or hell in one lifetime. The various denominations believe in a physical death that will be reversed in the future when Christ returns and resurrects the righteous. With science, they say there is no knowledge of what happens after you die. Reincarnation gives hope of renewal, with life after life that beginnings come from the end. You could say that reincarnation is like a fresh start on your new journey in life. Reincarnation is the rebirth of a soul in a new body.

With science, there is controversy about where the soul goes when it is between bodies? Where is the evidence of where the souls exist during their waiting time for their next incarnation? When we incarnate most people have no memory of their past life. Many questions come up from all these scientists looking for proof to accept only research that has reproducible results.

There are many cases documented of young people giving their parents their name in their past life. They also know where they lived and what they did in their past life. My ex-boss Rami, told me of a member in his family who remembered who he was in his past life and gave proof of it. People who live in India would pay attention to their young children when they tell their parents who they were before they came to them in the present life. The Indian parents would listen with great intensity to who their child stated they were previously. Many cases have been documented due to names, places and other information given to prove the child's past life.

I believe that reincarnation and faith are both considered where science needs proof to claim any breakthrough of whatever it is. Past life regressions are evidence of an altered state of the mind that is reached through hypnosis. Some people believe past life regressions represent proof of reincarnation. I would say the scientists have lived life with blinders on. Then again, I am no scientist.

Regressions are valuable because they help people understand themselves. I found that there are many cases of people who go to a regression hypnotherapist for answers to a serious they have. When the regressionist puts them under hypnosis, a past life gives them a very good reason for their problem. While you are being regressed, part of you is hypnotized and part is not. You have a dual state of consciousness. When you know and find out the truth about whatever you experienced in your past, it sets you free to leave it behind. To understand your fear and why it came into your life to begin can affect your mental and physical well-being.

Years ago, you would never find an article on reincarnation like this one. Two out of three people today in the West believe in reincarnation. This shows us that reincarnation is finding its way back to us.

This article I am referring to is one sent to me from my mother, Eva, and I cherish it today. The article was from a Unity Magazine in Providence, Rhode Island, which is a Christian magazine. I need to give recognition to Andrew B. Carlson for this precious article on reincarnation in March of 1986.

HOW MANY TIMES have you lived?

Is this your first appearance on the stage of life? Or have you lived five, ten, a hundred, or a thousand times before?

Many people believe that God has given us just one chance, just one opportunity to make the grade, to earn our spiritual crown. They say that if we fail to evolve spiritually, we are finished, that at the end of this existence, we either go up or down, depending on the kind of life we have lived. We either ascend to heaven or we descend to eternal hell and damnation. One chance is all! If you don't make it in this life, you've had it!

This is the extreme view of many. Would you be so intolerant that you would grant only one chance to another person, especially your own child? Few people would be that malicious. How then can we think that a loving God would treat us so despicably?

It seems to me that God has said, "Here, my child, I am going to grant you another chance; in fact, I'm going to give you as many opportunities as you need to rise to the spiritual standard that I have set for you. So, I will provide you with another human body in which you can continue to learn and grow."

This theory is called reincarnation, I say "theory," for this is what it is at the present time. But it seems to be a reasonable assumption. Reincarnation simply means the rebirth of the soul in a new human form.

Let us use a simple illustration. A man who has no knowledge of an automobile buys a car. But because of his mechanical ignorance, he forgets to put oil in the motor, and he lets the radiator run dry. In a year, the car is worn out and he trades it in for a new one.

By this time, he has learned a little about automobiles, and this one lasts him two years. Then, he trades it in for a third car, and with his mechanical knowledge constantly increasing, this car lasts him several years.

The same thing applies to reincarnation. Because of ignorance of spiritual laws, we have to lay aside our worn-out bodies, and trade them in for new ones. But this process of reincarnation eventually comes to an end. It stops when there is no longer a need for it. When we enter into the consciousness of Jesus Christ, the need for reincarnation ceases.

In his epistle to the Romans, Paul said: ...the whole creation has been groaning in travail together until now; ...as we wait for ...the redemption of our bodies. (Rom. 8:22, 23) Apparently, Paul was aware of the necessity to redeem the body from death and the grave.

The pure, incorruptible substance of Spirit must be allowed to penetrate and invigorate every cell and atom of our bodies. This is accomplished through pure, Christ-like thoughts and words. A good affirmation to use is: The life of God in me is untouched by time or age or any negative condition. In this life, I am continuously revitalized and renewed.

Thus, through different stages of reincarnation, gradually, the body becomes incorruptible and eternal. The thought of reincarnation comforts me. I am grateful to God for giving me another chance. Because, frankly, I wouldn't want to stand before the "judgment seat" today and have my soul weighed and balanced. I don't think that I have yet earned a permanent passport and visa into the kingdom of heaven. There is still much for me to learn before I can earn permanent citizenship in that fourth dimensional realm.

However, when I have grown sufficiently spiritually, I will have surpassed the need for reincarnation. It will have served its purpose for me. How will I know when I have reached this point in spiritual development?

I will know because I will have overcome selfishness, pride, fear, hatred, sickness, and other shortcomings. I must rise above all these adversaries before I outgrow the need for reincarnation. However, there is a final enemy to overcome: death. Paul said: The last enemy to be destroyed is death. (I Cor. 15:26) In other words, we shall continue to reincarnate until we have evolved to the place where we have overcome death.

In his book, Talks on Truth, Charles Fillmore said: When you refuse to receive this baptism of the Holy Ghost (or when you refuse to be receptive to principles of divine truth), your flesh is not quickened, and it must eventually go back to dust. In that case, you are again sent to school to learn the lesson in another earthly experience.

He adds: The goal of man is eternal life, and in each incarnation that goal is brought nearer if Spirit is given an opportunity to express itself. When this is done, the true spiritual body will replace the physical body and all men will become like Jesus Christ.

Bit by bit, reincarnation; after reincarnation, we evolve from our spiritual center to the circumference, until we become new creatures in consciousness and in the body. As a consequence, we will no longer need to go through the experience called death.

Through the assimilation of divine ideas of truth concerning eternal life, our bodies are becoming so refined that ultimately, they will disappear from the sight of those who see with the eye of sense; or with the physical eye only.

I believe that we are ultimately from this plane of existence in the full bloom of our lives, just as Jesus was, without having to experience the weakness and debility commonly associated with old age.

In this state of spiritual maturity, we will rise to a higher plateau of existence, which is physically invisible to us at our present level of understanding.

Our departure from this plane will not be death, as we think of it. It will be a journey taken by those who have graduated to this point, or this experience. It will be a journey similar to the ascension of Jesus Christ. We will be joined later by loved ones and friends as they progress to this same point of graduation.

When we come to see and understand this truth, as John says in Revelation 21:3, 4: "...God himself will be with them; he will wipe away every tear from their eyes, and death shall be no more, neither shall there be mourning nor crying nor pain any more, for the former things have passed away." This is the end of the article and I hope you received wisdom from it as I did.

I believe all things cannot be taught in just one lifetime. None of us are Jesus Christ, so there is a lot for everyone to learn. There are so many who teach us if we want to explore our many lives of the soul, we carry from one lifetime after another. I find this topic of reincarnation an eye-opener, as I always try to seek the truth, even though most of the Christian churches reject it.

Long ago, I think reincarnation was taken out of the churches due to a power structure for the church to be able to control you. Astrology used to be affiliated with religion and after a duration of time, there was a separation process by the church. Many famous people used astrology as a tool to assist and guide you on your path. You could say the same with reincarnation as a valuable tool to unlock that door to heal you from your fears and give you wisdom you seek.

I found "Healing Your Past Lives," by Roger Woolger, Ph.D., fascinating. Included in his book was a CD giving five guided regression exercises to access your past-life memories. These exercises help you to release old wounds and illuminate your life's purpose. I found these exercises enlightening while I was able to be comfortable at home to go deep within my soul to regress.

Roger stated IF WE REALLY WANT to know who we are, we must first know who we were.

Edgar Cayce is well known in his writings giving credence to the idea that past lives can contribute to illness, emotional difficulties, relationships, and so on. Cayce channeled thousands of past-life readings while in a trance state, even though his fundamentalist Christian conscious self-did not initially believe in past lives! Thanks to Cayce, many people now understand the idea of karma as the spiritual fallout of good or bad behavior from the soul's past.

You also have the Hindu teachings and the Dalai Lama and so many more to teach us about reincarnation and how to meditate. The making of a film like Little Buddha, with its story of a Tibetan lama reborn in the body of a young American boy, would have been unthinkable in Hollywood a generation ago.

At eighty-eight, Benjamin Franklin wrote to a friend: "I look upon death to be as necessary to the constitution as sleep. We shall rise refreshed in the morning." Many Westerners believe in reincarnation and evidence exists in the writings of poets, writers, and philosophers across centuries: William Shakespeare, Johann Wolfgang von Goethe, Walter Scott, Ralph Waldo Emerson, Emily Dickinson, Carl Jung, Winston Churchill, Norman Mailer, David Hume and Shirley MacLaine. The list goes on and on.

From the perspective of past-life therapy, none of this is surprising: the things we fear---fire, drowning, guns, explosions, savage animals, enclosed spaces, crowds, airplane trips---are not childhood traumas at all, but psychically inherited fears, residues of previous lives still carried deeply in the psychic system we call the unconscious or the soul. The horrors we most fear really happened to someone else, but that "someone else" is still in us today, an imprinted memory from a lifetime that is over, even if the past-life personality does not know it.

Raymond A. Moody, Jr. M.D. In his book, "Coming Back," gives us a great description of a past-life regression. Some people believe that hypnosis can tap an area of the brain that stores all or part of the lives they have lived like a file cabinet stores old tax records. This process of hypnotically getting at these past lives is called past-life regression.

Mr. Moody states, another great insight with regressions is that, when we regress, not everyone is famous. Some people would like to think they were Christopher Columbus, Abraham Lincoln or Cleopatra or some other famous historical figure. Most of the people who are regressed are ordinary people who were soldiers, slaves, gladiators or farmers. They were ordinary people living ordinary lives as in their present life. Not many people lived a life of grandeur.

In my past-life I was an ordinary Egyptian person who wanted to travel when I was young. The bright light was meeting Jesus during my travels. He is the reason my life became so dramatic and exciting. I wrote down what he preached and spread the news of this famous man named Jesus. Not only did I spread the news, but I became a follower without even knowing it right away. I got caught up in the Spiritual movement of all time history! I was hours away from being thrown in the Roman arena to be killed for being a Christian. A Roman friend set me free from the Roman arena and I flew back to Egypt to spread the word of Jesus Christ.

It was not who I was during that lifetime, but who I stumbled across during my travels. I was blessed to meet Jesus at that particular time and have been shown how important love is. Without this meeting for me, I would have been just an ordinary person traveling. In essence, you could say I was a small part of the greatest story ever told. Being at the right time and place was the most important and memorable past-life for me.

I remember when I met Peter Woodbury with the Edgar Cayce A.R.E., who has facilitated many regressions, that most of the time people gravitate back to their most dramatic lifetime they had. It would depend upon the individual, as some would speak through their regression and some were silent. Then, you had others who just felt peace and love surrounding them. Regressions are not all the same, as I found out for myself with two regressions I had with Peter. I also enjoyed a group regression with Peter that spurred me on with a private regression the next day. That regression was the best medicine I ever received with knowledge and words from my soul.

In my first regression, I spoke and told a story of who I was and what happened to me. In my second regression, I could not speak and realized that my mouth had been covered due to a long journey across the desert. It was interesting, as I tried to speak and felt like I was muzzled. I muttered out, but could not speak, as a cloth was wrapped around my whole face for protection from the wind and sand in the desert. If it had not been for that cloth wrapped around my face, I am sure I would have spoken a few words.

I am an avid believer of reincarnation and regressions. Through my spiritual journey here, I understand who I was and who I am today and why I received my "automatic writing through spirit" gift. I became a messenger for Jesus Christ during his time on earth and I am proud to be his messenger today in my book, "Your Soul's History."

CHAPTER 5

BASIC ROOTS

W e are now in my present life which begins in 1953, and I have left my Egyptian past life behind. All this time of history in my soul, needs to be connected to make sense and give answers. The wisdom of the past has been established and we shall see faith, love, and truth enter in now. Don't be afraid to unlock that door to connect everything.

As a young child, I awoke to see that the day coming in would be a typical weather day in New England. Rainy days here are plentiful, but so are the trees, grass, and flowers enriched with the added beauty derived from our weather. Mind you, we have sunshine also, and it is very welcome when it comes.

To live life on Cape Cod is a treat for a child who sees reality as a way of living. The old-timers sit and talk and tell their sea stories, while the children listen with great delight. The ocean is a gem, to be close to, and the art of shell fishing, along with fishing, is unique in this area. To be able to have the history of the past unfold, and yet, continue on for every child, is a blessing.

The villages on the Cape are unique in the sense that all the roads find their way to the ocean waters with style. The beauty of the area is how everything is structured. No set pattern ever appears to be like the layout of other parts of our beautiful country. The charming Cape has always been written and sung about.

Through the eyes of a child, the four seasons represented a fulfillment of joy. The energy was high for every child as spring brought more freedom to do different things in the area of entertainment. With our abundant rain in the spring, the flowers budded out, and little creatures awoke from their long winter sleep, along with the new growth of the leaves sprouting and showing their brilliance. Never would there be a better time for smelling the fresh air as when the winter gloom of coldness left us, allowing us to spread our wings like the birds that shared our delight in having warmer rays from the sun.

Outside activities were abundant, with bicycles along the sides of the canal and joggers coming out to run, while sharing the beauty of our famous Bourne and Sagamore Bridge.

During the summertime, everyone shines on the Cape, along with the sun. People from all over the world vacation with us as we are known for our tourism, as well as making everyone feel at home. There is no better time for swimming, sailing in and out of the harbor, or visiting with fellow sailors and listening to their tales of the day. Sailboats fill the ocean with adventures who love the wind behind their sails, to experience, time after time, the splendor of summer days and glorious sunsets of the summer nights. Famous clambakes on the beach are talked about the rest of the year. My favorites were the clam cakes or fritters you could buy and eat right on the beach. There is nothing like shellfish fresh out of the sea. I remember going clamming with my dad, assisting him by adding a few clams myself. Such wonderful memories came with the good smell of the fresh salt air, I sometimes took for granted.

As the sun slipped away more, we fell into my most favorite of seasons, known as the falling of the leaves. Before any leaves fell, beautiful sights of all different colors feasted our eyes, with no end to their beauty. This particular season always made me feel so alive inside, before the dead of winter would sneak in. The cool crisp air was wonderful to breathe in, and gave you a tingle inside to know that life was wide open, thanks to God's gift of nature surrounding us. When all the colors had vanished from the leaves, I knew that wintertime was coming upon us.

The winter season represented so much to a variety of people, both younger and older. Of course, the young, and some of the older athletic sorts, would appreciate the first fall of snow so their dusty skis could be used again. Several locations in New England would pack in herds of snow-lovers for the duration of the winter. Frozen-over lakes and small ponds were in demand for others who enjoyed their fancy footwork on the ice. This did not cost as much as going to the mountains, but it had the same impact as being outside in the cold, with the sparkling snow everywhere you looked, as you skated on the lake. The less adventurous individuals would find a good-sized fireplace and stay inside, sipping away on their hot toddies and enjoying interesting conversations with each other. As you age and your body says "no," you realize you can still walk outside and feel old man winter, for a small duration of time anyway.

During the winter months, house parties brought out skills in certain games, such as the art of pool, and board games, and many other entertaining sources of fun for others to share. Last but not least, that fireplace at night would take you into the stillness of time, where your thoughts of the day could unwind through silent meditation.

While others clear across the country lived a completely different lifestyle, this was the way the people spent their time during the four seasons on the Cape, as well as other New England states. The East has always been known for its excellent prize-winning seafood, with restaurants galore offering all your favorite treats from the ocean, cold-water treasures teasing your taste buds.

From the very beginning of Cape Cod to the very tip of Provincetown, you will experience the charm and see the beauty of the coastline, with every season giving you a variety of history beyond belief, along with the feeling of our forefathers long ago. It is as if you have gone back in a time machine while you are still in the present.

Starting life as a young child was quite different for me than for most children, as I would encounter a long battle with a rare kidney disease. This would be the beginning of many tests of faith where God made me aware of why I was born and showed me that I would need to struggle for many years throughout this lifetime.

At the tender age of three-and-a-half, my father found me lying on the cold cement outside of my grandfather's house, where it was a little cooler for me, as I was burning up with a high fever. I was rushed to a hospital close by in Wareham, but very little could be done for me there. My parents were advised to take me to Massachusetts Children's Hospital in Boston, and this hospital would become my new home for the next eight months.

This particular health problem was not a simple problem for a young child to have. It turned out to be a very rare kidney disease. There was no way I could return home, because my illness had not yet been discovered. Patience would become my first lesson.

People on the Cape donated money for my operation, as my parents with five other children to take care of at home, could not afford the huge expense. I was the only daughter, and my five brothers eventually became jealous, since all of my parents' attention was focused on me. A lot of time was spent driving to Boston where the doctors experimented on me in an effort to get to the bottom of what was causing my problem, therefore taking time away from my brothers.

The Cape Cod Times wrote several articles about me, and there was a picture showing me with my mother and the bag I needed to wear on my leg so I could urinate. After much prodding with needles and various tests, I had my first operation. Many prayers were said for me, and hopes were high that the operation would correct my kidney disease.

There was no success with this first operation, so it was back to the hospital in Boston, and it seemed as though I was being used as a guinea pig. I remember my dad busting through the doors because he heard me crying while the doctors used various needles on me. After additional research, the doctors tried the second operation. This operation was successful, and I no longer needed to wear a bag on my leg.

Praise God, my doctors performed the first kidney operation, wherein a new tunnel was made, allowing my urinary tract to be moved, allowing my urine to flow in a normal tract instead of backing up. It was like having a built-in detour. Because of this new opening, other problems followed throughout my life, and there were difficulties that the doctors did not foresee in my future. Their primary concern was to keep me alive. I believe God guided them, and they were able to save me. I made medical history and became the first female to go through this rare kidney surgery.

As it turns out, a cousin of mine also had this dreadful ailment, which turned out to be hereditary, but my parents gave the names of my doctors to her parents, and the operation was performed on her with success. I believe the doctors' first experimental surgery interfered with my female organs, and caused problems for me for the rest of my life. My cousin, from what I understand, was able to have a child, and was spared the agony of being childless throughout her life.

Can you imagine the worry, the heartache of having a young child so ill, and how my illness affected my parents' and brothers' lives? The bond I shared with my parents throughout this difficult time helped me to realize the powerful love we shared.

After the operations were over, my young life opened up, and I was able to venture out and explore more of the world. There would be no more stuffy hospitals where people came in and out of my room at all times of the day, or being taken out by doctors for one thing or another. It was time for me to be free like a bird, so I could fly wherever I wanted to go.

Acquiring freedom like that was a new beginning for me, and I was able to live the rest of my life in a normal fashion. I was able to play like the other children. It was not that I didn't appreciate the nurses and doctors trying to save my life, but I was a very young child, just four years old, and I didn't want to be caught up in the reality of my illness one second longer!

Back to visit with my grandfather Paradise (my mother's father) once again, on a much happier note, this time with no high fever to contend with. During one of my ventures out to play, I was in the cranberry bogs close by. This day has remained in my memory as a typical day out, with an adventure my parents could deal with, a normal situation for a young child to encounter. My older brother was close by and found me lying in the cranberry bogs in a nest of mad hornets. The hornets had gotten all stirred up. I had invaded their territory. They chased after me with great passion, and I was stung all over.

While I was running away, I was screaming, and my brother Bobby helped me take my blouse off, as the hornets were all inside my clothes, and we both proceeded to run further away from their anger. That situation would have been perfect for one of those "funny" moments on candid camera.

Needless to say, that was the end of our adventure for that day, but there was a little unexpected pleasure to come. After my parents realized what a mess, I had gotten myself into, it was quick mud-making time to soothe all of those bites the mad hornets had given me. I was rewarded with an ice cream cone after I was covered with mud, and I sat outside licking my ice cream, smiling and thinking how this certainly topped a day in the hospital with all those needles.

My homecoming was filled with other adventures which made me feel like any other little girl growing up with five brothers to play with. These memories can never be taken away from me, as I try hard to remember the happier times as a child. I have come to the realization that my hospital experience was a necessary element for my future, which would be filled with spiritual gifts to share with others as needed.

Growing up on the Cape provided a certain way of life, and we all took for granted the beauty of the land. We have had writers come and live on the Cape so that they could acquire the feeling that was prevalent amongst all of us, that our history was in our blood. Some of the history touched the souls of the people, because without our history, there would be no true understanding of our ancestors unwavering faith in God to protect them and guide them to new territory, where their belief system in worshipping God would be free and natural for every man and woman.

Cape Cod is a very romantic place, with sand dunes that stretch along the coastline. Brave men and women chose to cross the sea to experience whatever would come their way, in order for them to realize their dreams of new lands and the love of a new country, which their God supplied them with.

The history of family land became a mutual interest between my father and me, as he explained the history of our ancestors, who owned land on the Cape from the early 1600s. Generation after generation placed a mark in our U.S. History books, and we were related to these famous ancestors named the Perrys. To come from roots like that made us proud, knowing that our ancestors came from the Mayflower, and knowing what they had accomplished. The Town of Bourne office is on a street named Perry Avenue, after our famous ancestors, where all our tax money goes for town revenues.

Our family owned a 23-acre parcel in Bourne, Massachusetts, known as the woodlot, which was located in a small village. The primary reason my father wanted me to save the land which was passed down with great love for the history of the Perrys -- my grandmother was a Perry on my father's side – was also a fact that it was the meeting place of my mother, Eva, at age eight, and my father, Richard, who was 16 years of age.

My parents could not have known, as children, they would end up getting married. Two acres away from the family woodlot is where my mother lived as a young child, and it was there she saw my father for the very first time on his Harley motorcycle. He was sixteen years old, and was riding with a friend on my dad's motorcycle. They used my mother as the lookout girl for the police so they could cut across County Road, due to the fact they had no valid driver's license.

Years later, they found each other again, and they were married on the Cape. For several years, they lived in the two little houses next to the woodlot, until my father built the house by the fire station in the small village. I believe our friends, the Berry's, still live there, where my father built his first house many years ago.

The fond memories held in my heart for the history of the Cape were instilled in my soul during the many walks with my father, throughout the years, on the woodlot. All the history was told to me by my father with great admiration for our forefathers, who endured many adventures on the sea. These memories can never be taken away from me, unlike the land which was stolen from me by a corrupt developer, who used town officials to acquire the land along with greedy relatives, who received crumbs in the end for doing his evil bidding.

I was caught in a trap, for over eight years, as the greedy developer created a stronghold in that village to reach his goal of acquiring more land to better his position in the town. I had been released from the largest trap in my life, and I know that I gave everything in my heart and soul toward this endeavor of fulfilling a promise I gave to my father right before his death.

Everything went into applying all the elements I possessed from God, and even I could not fight all these evil greedy people who sought to steal this precious land my father asked me to fight for. The great love was established with one test after another. At no time did I give up, until I could try no more. All those trials let my father know I kept my promise to him, and throughout all of the attempts to win the land, I would receive, in the end, rewards from God which few people ever acquire.

While you read one chapter after another, the gift that God has bestowed upon me with my automatic writing will truly amaze you, as I never had this gift until the darkness began with all this evil surrounding me. To take on such a powerful enemy would have made any normal person want to run for the hills, but instead, I charged on for more until I could no longer fight. The incredible gifts from God kept me energized to continue on, and I prayed that I would be released from this trap of hell.

With the turn of events in the future, I ended up in California, and my father moved to the West to be closer to me. I sought an attorney in Massachusetts, prior to my father's death, to seek out how to get a handle on this legal web of greed.

CHAPTER 6

HISTORY BEYOND BELIEF

The history of our family is in U.S. History books today, which stems all the way back to the Perrys of the 1600s. To come from roots like that makes me proud, knowing my ancestors' names and what they accomplished. The Perrys were God-fearing people, and they chose to teach their children the way of the sea. They were taught from their fathers as very young children to be groomed to eventually become captains of their own ships. This is what they knew best, so teaching came very easy, to show their offspring the beginning stages as they remembered it.

As a son, it was simply laid out for the young boy in order to learn whatever his father knew, and thankfully, it was a lot. In time, he would be taught all of the skills of a sailor, with the sea also being a stern teacher, and he would learn how to turn the ship around, when fate from the ocean would meet the challenge of his very own life, along with all of his crew. As father and the sea taught the young man, the more confident he would become in the South Eastern part of the Cape.

The very first thing the lad would learn was respect for his ship, and to guard it with his life. That was the number one rule to learn. Without his ship, he had no home. His eyes needed to be sharp in order to watch for anyone and anything approaching without a warning, so it could be determined what the next step would be. As time transpired, all the laws needed to be learned, and he would be tested time after time, until the knowledge was just secondhand to the lad.

Eventually, the young lad became an old sea captain who told many sea stories, and he never forgot the rough weather he contended with, as his faith in God showed him the way to overcome the mighty challenges of the sea. There was also glory from the sea with the fish, whale meat, oil, and everything else derived from the famous whale.

Now we shall read about these courageous men and women who brought their suffering to bear, along with our famous history, which we shall never forget, as our roots have made us who we are today.

In the early 1600s, one of the first families was the Perry family, who sought refuge from a place that no longer held their hearts to stay where their roots were. These people were sea-faring people who had great faith in God. They had so much faith that a decision was made to leave their homeland and go to the sea, into uncharted waters.

Children and women were included in this trip, which was highly unusual. These God-fearing people chose to escape their persecutors, who were going to force them into a new order of their belief system. New information regarding God would be forced upon them, which would test their belief in God.

A decision was made, which was unanimously voted in, to set sail for a new world. They stood and sought approval from God to leave their worldly treasures behind, to escape with their belief system as they knew it.

Striking out into bold and cold waters with women and children was not a common act. Much angst regarding their families meant that it was all or nothing for the early Pilgrims to come to the new world known as Plymouth. Embarking upon this high-risk game of life or death, they laid their great faith in God to guide them to personal freedom.

Preparation started with the food they would need for any great length of time, so dry goods was paramount. The first several days of the voyage, they would have their best meals, for this was when they would still have perishables.

In the 1600s, the only real form of transportation was a ship. To sail a ship for any great distance meant you needed to be a well-seasoned sailor. Life on the high seas was not as romantic as most people thought, especially in the 1600s. The building of a ship was an art, indeed. These ships were on the crude side, but built with an aura of steadfastness. Whatever material the people had to build with was used with great precision, because the sailors had no other home like their well-made ships to carry them from one port of storm and upheaval to another.

In a sense, their ships were like their mothers, protecting them from all the dangers of the sea, and there were always rough seas to contend with during those days. Of course, they repeatedly asked God to guide them safely to wherever their destination may be.

Most ships were given women's names, to protect and guide them, as if the spirits from above watched over all of them. To be a sailor meant you sought out adventure and were courageous, with a thirst to explore and seek new worlds, and sometimes, a different course came into the picture when their compass lost its way. To sail off course due to a storm meant the adventure could potentially bring enemies with no love for these foreigners.

The Pilgrims didn't realize that the soil they walked upon would lead the majority into the deep earth forever. Many would perish in search of their personal freedom. To remain in England would have been even worse than death to those who gave themselves to this New World.

Throughout their lives, the remaining ones would form colonies, which would extend a great distance, with time on their side. The wisdom and strength to go on, due to their prayers and desire to seek a better world continued.

Yes, the Indians were their friends, and they assisted them through the first winter. Then, other Indian tribes decided to kill the Pilgrims. The friendly Indians taught them to plant corn, so they could survive their cold winter. Many died and had no markers with their names left behind. The only true death records were recorded in the family bibles each Pilgrim family kept. Knowledge not given of the total deaths to the unfriendly Indians insured their safety.

This was the beginning. Many others followed the Pilgrims. Everyone basically knows the rest of the history of the Pilgrims, so now it is time to zero in on who the sea-faring Perrys were.

Several Perry families came to New England in the 17th Century, but the first Perry to come to Cape Cod was probably Mrs. Sarah Perry, a widow from Devonshire, who arrived with her children, Ezra, Edward, Margaret, Deborah and Hannah, and settled in Sandwich in about 1637. She died before June 8, 1659, and an inventory of her estate was made, and her son, Ezra, was appointed executor.

Edward Perry, called Edward the Quaker, born in approximately 1630, in England, married Mary Freeman sometime C. 1654. She was the daughter of Governor Edmund Freeman.

*In that year, an official, Thomas Tupper, was cited for neglect to marry Edward Perry and Mary Freeman. The trouble was that Perry, being sympathetic with the Quakers, declined services of either a clergyman or magistrate. For this offense, he also appeared several times before the court, and once again for rejecting the official services of the Governor, who, as a relative of the parties, had been requested by the court to see that the marriage be legalized.

In 1654, Edward Perry was fined *15 for disorderly marriage, and Magistrate Prence, while passing by on his return from Court to Eastham, wanted to marry him rightly.

Perry refused, and was told that his fine of *15 would be assessed every three months until he complied. (Pilgrim Republic, by Goodwin).

Edward Perry's fines under Quaker persecution were the heaviest in the Colony. In the year 1658, they amounted to L89-18 shillings and 17 head of cattle.

Edward fled to Rhode Island to escape fines and punishment in Sandwich, and found refuge with the Society of Friends in Providence Plantation, and built on the farm at South Kingston.

Edward Perry settled at Scorton, an east side village of Sandwich, and owned a large tract of land which included the Great Spring at Spring Hill. Sandwich was the first town on the Continent of America to establish a regular monthly meeting of the Society of Friends, which was set up in 1658. Edward Perry was the first clerk. He may be considered the first Sandwich author. His religious writings were published between 1676 and 1690. One of the titles was, "A Warning to New England and to the Court of Plymouth – This is the Word of God."

He died in Sandwich on February 16, 1696. This same year, the town gave to their neighbors, called Quakers, half-an-acre of ground for a burial place on the hill above Canoe Swamp and between the Ways. Edward Perry, in accordance with his Will, was buried at Spring Hill Burying Place, amongst his friends.

During the later 1700s and early 1800s, whaling became the most popular way to earn a good living, not to mention all the wonderful extras it brought to all of New England. Many men died during this time due to the difficulty in shooting the whales, which was not an easy feat, by any standard.

Tools were designed to assist the brave men who chose to hunt the big white whales. Harpoons were sharp and were fired out into the air to land in the whale's skin. One harpoon would not suffice in any one whale. It took hours to kill a whale, and many men were needed to tie the whale up and bring it in.

To finally bring home the treasures derived from the whale was considered a huge honor throughout the whole town. Men were blessed for their courage, and encouraged to go out again, so people could continue to have oil to burn for heat and light. Ivory from the whale's teeth was turned into Scrim Shaw used to make beautiful jewelry, with pictures of ships, and more art and beauty.

Whaling continued for many years, until new ways of living were discovered and brought to New England. As time went on, whaling expeditions were no longer as popular. Now, the young and middle-aged men needed to experience other interesting avenues, and an easier way of life.

It was in the 1890s that a new invention was on the horizon, bringing with it a new way to travel. No longer was there just a horse and carriage, or a train, but the car became the newest vehicle for transportation. What excitement for people to witness pieces of metal put together, with seats and a steering wheel! It was the talk of the town. If you were wealthy enough, you could go right out and purchase that wild piece of metal and go for a drive. No horse to whip to get things moving for you, because you were the driver, with gears to put you in different speeds to go faster.

Even if you were not rich, the time would come when the price of an automobile would go down, after the novelty wore off. Enough of these vehicles came off of a production line, making the price more affordable. Needless to say, the only thing a man could think about was how he would acquire enough money to own one of these automobiles.

As time passed, you could even purchase a used automobile, and that was the practical route to go. What did it matter how old an automobile was, as long as you had one to drive, instead of a horse and carriage?

The turn of the century was just around the corner, with many new devices soon to be invented. There was electricity in the air, and then lo-and-behold, whale oil was not needed as it once was. People could walk at night without carrying a candle. It was a new age of exciting inventions, one right after the other. The era of the whaling days of New England would soon be just a thought of the past, replaced with new roads filled with automobiles, and lights for those who did not need to rely on whale oil any longer.

A century later, another famous Perry was Christopher Perry, who continued in the merchant service for 12 years, and in 1798, was made port captain in the U.S. Navy.

The children of Christopher Perry were colorful, indeed, and they followed in their father's footsteps with a larger area to navigate in their sea-faring adventures. Oliver Hazard Perry, born in South Kingston on Aug. 23, 1785, married Elizabeth Champlin Mason.

Oliver entered the Navy as midshipman in 1799, and he served in the Tripoli Tan War. He had charge of the fleet on Lake Erie. In 1813, he met and captured the British squadron, and he sent the famous dispatch, "We have met the enemy and they are ours."

Perry was promoted to Commodore and received the thanks of Congress. In 1815, he commanded the Java in Decatur's squadron in the Mediterranean, and in 1819, he was sent to fight the pirates in the West Indies. He died in Port of Spain, in Trinidad, of yellow fever, and the date was August 23, 1819.

Matthew Galbraith Perry was born in Newport, Rhode Island, and in 1794, he married Jane Slidell. He was midshipman at 15, and he served in the War of 1812. He rendered important service while in command of Brooklyn Navy Yard, and was made Commodore in 1841. He was sent and aided in the capture of Vera Cruz in 1847. Next, he organized and commanded the expedition to Japan in 1853, and signed the treaty with the government in 1854, which opened Japan to western influence.

There you have the history of the famous Perrys, which completes the puzzle as to why continue on with this history that touched my father's heart and soul, and for me to promise my father, before he died, that I would fight for this precious land and name our family woodlot "Perry Estates."

Fortunately, the history involved in our family tree became of great importance to me while my father shared his knowledge and genealogy papers from my grandmother's trunk. At least the history of the sea-faring Perrys remains steadfast in our U.S. History books today. To know that no one can ever change or destroy those facts brings great comfort to my soul.

Another piece of Perry history was found recently in 2021 with proof of a negative of Schooner Charles Whittemore, while I went through some of my father's papers. I know my father guided me to find this negative through spirit, giving me the last sea story of the Perrys.' My father, Richard Curry, died in 1989 and wanted me to share this piece of exciting history. How could I not include this as I received another history lesson from my father? His history keeps coming even from the other side! I researched this ship and found an article from SEA CLASSICS in December 2017.

A four-masted schooner named the Charles Whittemore made history as THE TOP-SECRET DECOY. That was the name of the article written by Carol W. Kimball describing an ingenious scheme with plenty of excitement. This negative had the name written on the bottom and is the same picture in the article of the Schooner Charles Whittemore. This picture and article appeared for me, just like the mystery ship she was, preparing for strange secret missions.

USS Charles Whittemore was a four-masted lumber schooner used as a decoy ship against German U-boats during World War I. She was built by Michael B. McDonald and Sons of Mystic, Connecticut. She was launched on September 21, 1905, six weeks after McDonald's shipyard went into receivership. Her original owner was F> P. Boggs of Boston. Her first master was Captain Salathiel Henry Perry. She was originally employed in the lumber trade between South Carolina and Nova Scotia.

I remember my father telling me about this famous ship, and my great grandfather Captain Salathiel Henry Perry was in partnership with Mr. Whittemore. He owned a shoe polish company named after him. I would say his four-masted schooner was talked about more than his shoe polish.

Previous to her Navy hitch, the vessel sailed in the lumber trade nearly 13-years with Captain Perry in command. She was christened by Miss Eda Perry, the skipper's daughter, and named for a stockholder. This typical lumber schooner, 582-tons, 177-ft x 38-ft x 14-ft, sailed in October for

Georgetown, South Carolina, with a cargo of hard pine. On routine coasting trips, Captain Perry's wife Sara Jane Phinney, went along making the schooner their second home.

All went well until the 13th of March, 1918, when the lumber-laden Whittemore lost her rudder in a storm off Block Island, Rhode Island. No ocean tugs were available, so the owners applied to the Navy Communications Officer at Boston for a tow to port.

During July 1918, a battered four-masted schooner, the Charles Whittemore lay at anchor off the US Naval Training Station at Newport, Rhode Island. In the case of Charles Whittemore, it was decided that she would resume her role as an innocuous merchant ship in the hopes that she would become a target for U-boats. As Charles Whittemore was a relatively small sailing vessel, it was likely that a U-boat commander would not consider her worth a torpedo. Instead, it was hoped, a submarine would surface and attempt to sink Charles Whittemore with its deck gun. In anticipation of this eventuality, Charles Whittemore would be towing a submarine on the theory that the submarine could sink the U-boat before Charles Whittemore would be sunk.

USS Charles Whittemore was commissioned on 9 August 1918, with Lieutenant J. Lyons, USNRF, in command. The schooner cleared New London 15 August 1918 towing the submarine USS N-5 (SS-57) bound for the shipping lanes in the North Atlantic where it was hoped German submarines would attack a seemingly defenseless ship. Since no contact was made with the enemy, and N-5 broke loose during a storm. Charles Whittemore returned to New London on 9 September. She later conducted a similar mission with the submarine USS L-8 without encountering a hostile submarine.

Continuing her service with the Atlantic Submarine Force,

the Charles Whittemore carried submarine supplies, vital spare parts, and other cargo between New York, Newport, New London, Bermuda, and Charleston, S.C. until 14 May 1919 when she retuned to New York from Hampton Roads to be sold. She was decommissioned and transferred to her new owner 20 May 1919.

Charles Whittemore later was damaged by fire and a storm off Cape Cod on 11 January 1927, and abandoned at sea. This famous schooner served many people with lumber and historical secret missions during the war.

We all have history carried within our souls. I know who I am due to my past, to be able to move forward. It has taken me many years to put all of my pieces together, so I understand my true purpose of being here.

CHAPTER 7

AWARENESS TO SPIRITUALISM

After reading my introduction, you know that I was guided to a spiritualistic church. My mother was raised a Catholic, and after her first marriage at a young age, she divorced and became a Baptist. My father was raised a Methodist on the Cape, and my parents told me that I could visit other churches, if I chose to. I was invited to go to church with a Catholic friend, but I realized that the Catholic Church simply did not impress me. The priest was speaking Latin, and I could not understand the sermon, not to mention having to pay a quarter for my seat. That, in my humble opinion, was not conducive to attracting new members.

I also went to the Baptist Church as it was close to our house at that time. My father remembers vividly that I used to get up for church and I would walk, little white Bible in hand, through the snow-covered streets, to church. I did not want to miss singing in the choir, and I sang solos quite a bit.

During the summer, my younger brother, Jeoffrey, and I attended vacation Bible school at our church. We didn't know at the time, but what we were taught at that early age would stay within our souls the rest of our lives. More children should experience vacation Bible school, as it helps to keep spiritual nourishment flowing into adulthood. We would have less crime especially in the larger cities, where gangs and drugs are prevalent.

When I cried out to God and asked him to guide me to a church during my father's illness with cancer, I had no idea what a spiritualistic church was, or that one even existed. How could I know that in years to come, I would be able to give spiritual readings to people who truly needed answers from above for their peace of mind? To know that in the future, I would acquire a rare gift from God called automatic writing through spirit, was just not something in my realm of comprehension.

As time went on, I discovered that gifts from God were acquired through a special element called love, where anything is possible. Before my father died, I asked him to promise me that when he reached the other side, he would communicate with me. He said that he would, if he could. Those exact words came through my minister during a reading after my father's death.

While anticipating a private reading with my minister, as I drove into his driveway, I encountered a surprise. After I shut off my ignition, I rolled my window down more than half way, and a small sparrow landed right on my window. The bird's eyes stared into my eyes. The bird's eyes were a deep dark blue, just like my dad's. This intense stare lasted for about 30 seconds, and then the sparrow flew off the window and into the sky. I hurried out of my truck, looked toward the sky, and watched the sparrow vanish into the air.

I asked my minister about this incident that had just occurred. He said that my father had visited me in spirit. That the bird brought a special message of love from my father, who was basically telling me, "I am on the other side and communicating with you."

The Indians told stories of animals visiting their loved ones, while the spirit of that loved one was inside the animal, just so a presence could be observed and touched by the grieving individual. There again, the love element was shown to me, just as the Indians had experienced for centuries through their ancestors' teachings of spiritualism. The Indians were the first spiritualists on the North American continent, and still believe in their ancient ways.

Finally, my session began, and I had a myriad of questions for which I needed answers. I asked if my father would communicate with me again. The promise came through as I had requested before my father died, that he would communicate if he could. Well, I would have fallen down if I had not been sitting down already. I have never mentioned those private, exact words exchanged between the two of us to anyone.

More information came forth, using the terminology of a sailor, and I knew it was definitely my father talking from the other side.

Now my father was in heaven, and very happy to be rid of his cancer-stricken body, no longer suffering unbearable pain. Only love surrounded him in his current home on the other side. He said that his first priority was to keep a close eye on me always.

When you reach the other side, if you are high enough on your spiritual ladder, so to speak, you may watch over your loved ones. If you have not reached that spiritual level, then you may not protect your loved ones.

My father kept his promise to me, and I would keep the promise I made to him. He had requested of me, several months before he died, that I continue to fight for the property on the Cape, which we both paid taxes on since 1972.

At the time, I didn't know that my promise would bring on a state of ongoing depression, along with, at a much later date, the great joy of receiving spiritual gifts. Only through many trials and tribulations would these gifts be bestowed on me.

Unfortunately, this parcel of land called the woodlot, a 23-acre parcel located in, Massachusetts would require years of investigation on my part. The only heir to the land was my father, Richard Curry, who stepped forward and paid ten years of back taxes, going back to 1963. From that point on, no one else in the family had given one thought to the family woodlot that is, until my father requested his siblings sign over their shares to him. The other option was for him to file for adverse possession in 20 years.

At that point, one of his sisters, Mary, said that he could have her share, but he never received a written statement from her. The other two sisters, Marjorie and Eleanor, decided they wanted to keep their little shares. The funny thing was that none of them had ever offered to pay their small share of the taxes, when the land held no real material value, only historical and sentimental value, which was extremely important to my father.

After my grandmother, Amelda Perry Curry, died in 1953, my father found the family genealogy papers that were stored in her chest. All the siblings in the family went through their mother's personal items from her chest, before my father, who, being the youngest child, was the last one to see what was left. Several treasures were found by him, as the history of the exciting adventures of the seafaring Perrys unfolded right before his eyes. Along with all the genealogy papers was a shell with green and yellow mold covering it, and after cleaning the shell, there appeared the magnificent Lord's Prayer, which was etched on it. My father explained that throughout the whaling days, all the whalers spent a lot of time at sea, and they would pour acid on the artifacts and write in whatever they chose. A lot of jewelry was made from the whale's teeth, which was called scrimshaw, and sold throughout New England, many with various whaling sketches etched on them.

Everyone passed by all the family original history papers, as the different lines of genealogy meant more to my father than his siblings.

During the depression, my father's wish was to go to college and become a history teacher, but that was not to be. My father, instead, stayed with his mother and helped her, as his father had died when my father was only two years old.

Throughout the years, I contacted several attorneys in regard to the woodlot, but there seemed to be no simple solution. The original deed had been burned in a fire in 1840, along with many other papers, in Barnstable County. That meant the land would not be clear to seek title, unless an heir put in an offer to all the other heirs, and in the very end, a developer could step in and purchase the land. In our case, only one developer worked closely with the attorney and a real estate commissioner.

The woodlot meant a lot to me, because my father shared his knowledge of the land, and taught me where we came from, and who our ancestors were. It was as if I had my very own history teacher by my side, and each and every time we walked the land, there was a new history lesson given to me.

As time went on, I became fascinated with the unique characters in our family genealogy, and discovered how they brought so much to other people in southeastern Massachusetts, the famous, well-known part of Cape Cod.

Each year, my father and I sent our money to the Town Hall of Bourne for their tax revenues, and in the early 1980s, the land started to appreciate in value. At this time, I had convinced my father to join me in California. My father loved the Cape, but was divorced from my mother, and had just recently lost his friend, so he decided to move across the country to be closer to me.

The element of love we shared was so extreme that I questioned a lot of things at a later date, when I was introduced to the spiritual side of life. The closeness we felt was indescribable, and the more I studied spiritualism, along with knowledge of past-life times we shared, the more awareness I acquired in order to comprehend our element of love, which we held in such high regard.

As the years passed by, my father and I shared many joyous occasions. In 1985, we discovered that cancer had invaded his body, and we knew that time may not be our friend for too much longer.

With that knowledge, my father underwent radiation treatments. At that time, I was engaged to a man who had two small boys. I also worked a full-time job, and needed to be by my father's side. I eventually broke off my engagement and quit my full-time job. Time was of the essence.

I picked up a part-time sales job, in order to be able to work around my father's doctor appointments, radiation treatments, and pharmacy trips. I sacrificed a lot, but I would do it all over again, as I chose to be my father's caregiver for the duration of time he had left on this earth.

Death was something I had never experienced, involving someone so close to me. Although I had several brothers residing in California at that time, I had no support from them.

Fortunately, my youngest brother, Jeoffrey, flew in from Rhode Island and visited for a week or so, along with my mother, who stayed for three months. My parents had been divorced for many years, yet they were able to enjoy each and every moment together, because they still loved one another. They were both able to forgive each other of hurtful things from the past, and also reminisce about their happier memories of long ago. This was the best prescription of love for me, to be able to observe them laughing and enjoying their best three months ever together.

The departure time for my mother to go back to Rhode Island was most difficult for all three of us, as it would end our three glorious months together. Now the new enemy would be creeping back in.

Prior to my mother leaving, she strongly urged me to seek help, as she was afraid, I would have a nervous breakdown. My whole life was upside down, with nowhere else to turn but God. The world I once knew became very cold and dark and I realized then that several friends meant more to me, due to their constant concern, than my brothers who were close by, living in their own worlds, with little knowledge of the hurt I felt inside.

Every time I would have to leave my father by himself, I was paralyzed with fear inside of returning home. What would I find when I opened the door? I was so afraid of losing my very best friend, my loving father.

After being guided to my spiritualist church, information was given to me by my minister, through a reading that I would be in a lengthy lawsuit with my relatives. In April of 1992, it all began. But I had knowledge of it in 1986, after my father died, that a relative named Andrew or Peter would initiate the lawsuit.

My father's sister, Marjorie, in 1992, signed a petition to partition the 23-acre family woodlot in Massachusetts. My Aunt Marjorie's son, Peter, had previously sent papers to all the relatives giving us instructions to go in with a certain attorney, who would buy the land and develop it at a later date. I needed to give permission, as well, but I would not go along with their game plan, so the real estate law firm dropped their interest in my relatives.

I had full knowledge, in advance, concerning this upcoming event, and so I decided to study for a real estate license in order that I might acquire more experience in the real estate market. As it turned out, whatever knowledge or experience I may have gleaned from that endeavor was fruitless, as I was dealing with a corrupt group of people, and I was basically in a no-win situation. This journey would take me into a world of greed I could never encounter again in this lifetime, and I would see the ingenious level of treachery practiced by a developer, legal officials and relatives.

CHAPTER 8

DIFFICULT FAMILY TIMES

In the meantime, after my father's death in 1986, I went back East and stayed with my mother in Rhode Island for several months, as I was lost without my father. What better person to spend time with after such a loss than my other best friend, my mother? My nerves were on edge after watching my beloved father slipping away each day.

Yes, in reality, we are all dying each day we live on earth, but when cancer enters into your life, your time clock starts ticking out of control.

As the time factor enters your life, you realize what is really important. Time, does not stop for anyone, and whatever time is left is precious. As for myself, I took the time to show my father how much I cared by allowing him to step into my life with no limitations. In other words, I had much more time on my side, and felt that whatever time he had left, I would tune into his needs and happiness.

Many people cannot make that huge sacrifice, as they have families and need to work. I had no family to take care of, and

I dove into uncharted waters out of the great love I had for my father. With time, I understood why I chose to do what I did in a very special way, due to the spiritual connection of our shared past lives. To give from the heart is the most precious earthly gift you can offer someone.

Unfortunately, I had several brothers who did not share my feelings towards our father. That was their choice to make, as other elements of jealousy prevailed. I was left in charge of the fight for the land on the Cape, and words were spoken by one brother to my father, prior to his death, which were very hurtful to him, and unkind. The irony of it all was that I received very little money to help in my fight for our valuable land. In the end, I prevailed, with my sanity intact and held my head high, knowing I did exactly what was right in my heart and soul.

While visiting with my mother in Rhode Island during the fall of 1986, after my father's death, I asked my friends to drive me to the Cape. The old cow path, or cart path, was quite different now as I walked alone, but my father walked along with me in spirit. Dealing with grief takes a toll on an individual, and your body functions in ways you never experienced before. The loss of a loved one is so unbearable that you cannot even put your feelings into words, as the loss is so deep and severe that you secretly wish you could die also to be close to that loved one again.

On one particular morning, when my mother left to do some volunteer work, I was alone for the first time since my arrival in Rhode Island. While I was lying on my mother's bed, I finally released my feelings and cried for a long time. I missed my father so much, I thought I would break like a China doll. Suddenly, there was this great warmth of energy that engulfed me. I knew instantly it was my father who had come through spirit to comfort me, and he gave me his love vibration, telling me that "Everything will be all right honey bunch." Those exact words were given to me by my father whenever I was upset with anything when he was alive.

After receiving that awesome energy, I got right up and felt much better. To grieve is such a traumatic element of life, but I felt grateful that my father had communicated with me. Grief comes in many different ways, as you cry, become angry, and often times, deep depression sets in and you just can't quite shake the sense of loss.

With time, I understood more about spiritualism, year after year. The more I learned, the more aware I became of just how much more is happening in our universe than we know. Other mysteries of life exist beyond our exterior of living, and much greatness of the love element that is connected with God, is present in a very simplified manner, for all to understand the beauty and concept from a higher vibration. The simplicity of receiving information from the other side is just like an individual turning on a television, or a car radio to listen to music or a talk show.

Therefore, while you practice meditation more and more, your frequency with the other side gets sharper with time, and you receive information and sometimes become a medium. When you are able to tap into this new channel of love, it becomes easier to know and realize that your loved one that has departed is in that higher place, where nothing but love surrounds them in heaven.

The loss of a loved one, whether through an accident, cancer, heart attack, or old age, leaves us with a feeling of tremendous grief. We are of the flesh, and we miss the human body that served its way around on our earth plane.

After experiencing my father's death in 1986, and grieving for him for over a year, I received a phone call from my brother,

Jeoffrey, in Rhode Island, who informed me that our beloved mother had cancer. My mother could not call me, because she knew how difficult it was for me in dealing with my father's illness. At that time, my brother was residing in Rhode Island, not far from where my mother lived. Jeoffrey was always close with our mother and became her steady source of encouragement. The diagnosis was carcinoma of my mother's stomach.

Receiving the news of my mother's illness made me realize that you just never know what life has in store for you. Again, just a little over one year from my father's passing, and the horror strikes my mother. Cancer is so prevalent in our society, and it seems no one is immune from it.

There was a lump the size of a lime, above my mother's stomach area, which needed to be removed. Surgery was necessary if she wanted to try to live longer, and we prayed that all the cancer could be removed. There are never any guarantees when you open someone up. My brother, Jeoffrey, and I talked our mother into having the surgery. We did not want to lose her, and we were quite selfish with our wishes. In the end, she agreed and decided to have surgery. At the time, our mother, Eva, was 65 years old. She was cut from under her breast, all the way up to her back shoulder. She was brave and strong in her faith and believed that she would make it through surgery.

After surgery, the doctor told me that it did not appear as though he had gotten all the cancer. I cried, knowing this, and I wondered how much time she had left. It would be a little over two more years for her to be with us.

My mother awoke after the long surgery and asked me what was wrong, as I had been crying for a while. "What is wrong, Sandra?" she asked. I couldn't lie, and I told her that the doctor didn't think he had gotten all the cancer.

The surgery that was performed removed two-thirds of my mother's esophagus, which is needed in order to digest food. Therefore, her ability to eat and digest food properly dwindled away, because of the pain she suffered after each meal.

As time went on, my mother lost 80 pounds, which was half of her body weight. Eventually, the carcinoma of her stomach invaded her frail body, and slowly, she suffered the torture of this dreaded disease.

In the winter of 1988, I convinced my mother to come and stay with me in California for several months. She made fun of her appearance, and said that she looked like a dried-up California raisin on the front of a cereal box, and that she just might fit in fine where I lived. I told her to come out, no matter how she looked, and assured her that our warm rays of sunshine would be great for her health, rather than the cold New England winter. That did the trick.

Upon my mother's arrival at the airport in San Diego, the reality of her illness hit me like the wind of a hurricane. I found her sitting in a wheelchair, waiting for me. All I could do was try to hide my horror at seeing how her body had dwindled away, and I wrapped my arms around her with great love. The wheelchair assisted me in hiding my tears, as I pushed her over to the baggage claim area. She was making funny little jokes about herself to try and make light of her appearance. I was so happy she had come to be with me, so we could spend precious time together.

Even as I write now, tears stream my face as I think back on how much she suffered. After settling in at my home, we went to church every Sunday night and Friday for a healing class held at my spiritualist church. There were classes on Wednesday nights for spiritual understanding, and on Friday evenings, healing classes. Every Sunday evening, before church service began, you could acquire a healing by just going up to the front and sitting on a healing stool. Eva, my mother, did not hesitate, and gladly sat on the stool to receive her healing. Every Friday and Sunday night, for three months, healings were given with great energy by the minister and other healers of the church.

During my mother's visit with me, she gained nine pounds, and we all held onto hope for the future. In April of 1989, she flew back to Rhode Island so that she could enjoy springtime in New England.

Several months later, my brother Jeoffrey called to tell me that her cancer had returned. My mother mentioned that all the healings at my little church in California had helped her tremendously, and that she may have been healed, if only she could have stayed with me to continue on with healings twice a week.

Unfortunately, at the time, my mother lived in a low-income senior housing unit, and she didn't want to lose her benefits in Rhode Island. We were told that it could take up to five years in California to receive the same benefits.

Meanwhile, Jeoffrey called me in late August of 1989, to say that our mother was in the hospital, and that she was dying. My brother cried and told me that he could not go through this alone.

Another brother, Wayne, was visiting with me at the time, and he got on the phone and tried to encourage Jeoffrey to hang in there the best he could. Wayne wanted to assist more, as he was the closest with our mother as a younger child, but had little money of his own to offer at that time.

I called the hospital after Jeoffrey's frantic phone call and asked to speak with my mother. The nurse said that my mother had no phone in her room. I told the nurse that I needed to make a decision whether or not to put my personal items in storage and fly out to be with my mother. She and another nurse had to move my mother's bed up to the nurses' station so she could speak with me. My mother told me she was very impressed with the way I took control of the situation.

I asked her if she wanted me to come and stay with her. I knew her situation was grave, and she had little time left. My mother said, "You don't have to come," and I told her, "I will see you by next week." She told me that she would wait to see her sunshine again.

At this time in my life, I was selling real estate. It was the later 80s, and money was not exactly flowing my way. I asked none of my brothers for money. The reason I didn't ask my two brothers in California for their help was that they were too busy when our father died, and I had too much pride to ask them for anything after their selfish ways with our parents. They both knew what they did and what they didn't do to make things right, and everyone needs to face their own demons in the mirror. As for myself, I can look at both of their pictures in my home and feel grateful that I was there for them in their time of need, and I showed them unconditional love.

My old friend, John, came to my rescue, and he understood completely the situation I found myself in, with my mother dying in the hospital. He offered to buy me a ticket to Rhode Island, no questions asked. John still does not know to this day how grateful and indebted I am to him for being so generous and kind. Financially, I was at an all-time low in my life, and he came through so I could be with my mother.

Upon my arrival in Rhode Island, Jeoffrey picked me up and told me how relieved he was that I could be there with him during this painful time. My mother's doctor was extremely nice, and he released our mother from the hospital, under my care. At the time, I was not aware that the nurses and doctor had seen me visiting with my mother, and they told me that my love for her was very evident in the way I sat by her bedside holding her hand every day. For that reason, they released her from the hospital, so that she could be at home with us during her final days. Having a caregiver was crucial and a necessary component for the hospice program to be successful.

For almost six weeks, my mother required constant care, as different drugs were given to her at certain times, and everything had to be documented. As time went on, I started to develop bags under my eyes. My mother was comforted knowing that I was there to supply her every need, and my brother, Jeoffrey, was with us every night.

They started giving her morphine orally from a small cup. The next step was administering morphine through the tubes and the machine supplied by hospice, and at the end, morphine was given in a suppository form. I made sure she was in no pain, as I had a good supply. The hospital did run out of morphine for several hours, during her visit and I kept asking when it would arrive. I would not allow that to ever occur again!

There is nothing more tragic than to witness a loved one slowly dying before your eyes, and to realize that you cannot change the outcome. All I could do was remain steadfast by her side, until her last breath was taken. I remember both of my parents visiting me in the hospital when I was so sick. How could I not be there for them when they needed me the most?

Giving freely of our time for those we cherish is the ultimate gift of love. Instantly, the knowledge of impending death changes everything, and gives us a whole new meaning and perspective on life.

In essence, the bottom line is this: You may never walk the earth plane as you do now, and so, what is really important to you? What you once considered very meaningful to you has just been thrown into the trash and disregarded as foolish, and not worthy of even thinking about any longer. Your views have been subject to change in a big way, and you will act upon making serious changes that you never ever dreamed about before. This rings true for the individual afflicted with illness, as well as the loved one who remains on the earth plane. Therefore, so many people need to figure out what direction they will choose to go in.

Not all people deal with death in the same manner. Each individual has to make a choice; how close are you with this afflicted soul, and do you choose to look the other way, or does it just not affect your life the same way as it would with someone you truly care about? When you are the one who truly cares, then you make the choice to make a difference, while other family members can move on with their lives with no regrets, or maybe they carried guilt a few years down the road.

I have learned, after many years, and understanding more about spiritualism, to let go of the feelings I harbored against several of my brothers, as greed and jealousy entered into our lives. My greatest sadness is for my parents, because they wanted my brothers to reach out to them more before their time was up, perhaps visiting with them for the last time with no emotional turmoil, or to simply pick up the phone to say "I love you" for the very last time. The bitterness I held in my heart ate away at me, due to their selfishness prior to both of my parents' deaths.

My brothers should be grateful that I was the care giver to each of our parents. Taking time off from one's job is difficult, and becoming a private nurse is not an easy task, either. Fortunately, neither of my parents ended up in a nursing home. I have had little communication with three of my brothers, and just recently reconnected due to our brother, Wayne, who died in 2006.

Dealing with my bitterness was not something that came easy, and it was time I needed to be able to finally forgive them for their unkind acts toward our parents. I learned with studying spiritualism my understanding was to release all my bad energy towards them. Forgiving them would set me free, once and for all. I just recently forgave my cousin who ripped my heart out and heard he is financially set for life.

What good does it do me, when we are taught from the master himself to be able to forgive someone? If I am able to have a healthy relationship with my brothers, then so be it. They may have learned a few things during the many years I chose to be separated from them. We are all here to learn and grow spiritually. Sometimes it takes years and years to finally get it. I for one am stubborn and have a lot of pride.

When my brothers reach the other side, our father and mother will be there with open arms, and they will say they are sorry, and all shall be forgiven immediately. Within their hearts now, it could all be said, but some people don't bother until they reach those pearly gates and loved ones are there to greet you. How do you walk away from all those heavenly lights, with nothing but love surrounding you, and not be compelled to embrace the light and cleanse your soul? The other side brings out the good, and if there is a very bad affliction, then another lifetime may unfold to make a major spiritual lesson requirement.

CHAPTER 9

TRUE COLOR OF RELATIVES' GREED

Since 1972, my father, and I had continued to pay all of the real estate taxes on our 23 acres in a small village, located in the State of Massachusetts. Not one of our relatives gave one simple thought to have any of their money sent to the Town of Bourne for their share of the taxes, as an heir on this large piece of land.

My father did approach his three sisters and asked if they would sign over their shares to him, after he had saved the land from being acquired by the Town of Bourne. At the time, the value of the land was of no great amount, just sentimental value filled with generations of Perry history. My Aunt Marjorie and Aunt Eleanor stated they would like to hold onto their shares of land.

There was Aunt Mary, who said she had no interest in the land, and said that my father could have her share, but nothing was ever put into writing. A mere verbal statement held no substance in court. Needless to say, that did not help my father and me in the future, as her daughter received her percentage from the sale of the land many years later, along with other siblings.

After my father's death in August of 1986, I flew from California to Cape Cod to handle my father's probate and address legal problems with the land. While I spoke with my probate attorney in Bourne, he advised me to speak with the developer of the property abutting our family land. Little did I know at that time that my attorney's partner represented this developer, and would create havoc for me in the near future.

During October of 1986, I met with this developer on his land, right next to our family woodlot. He told me that he was a developer, and would like to purchase the land right next to his. He gave me his card and mentioned that he had a special permit on his land that would affect my land, which I could not change. I never felt comfortable around him, mainly due to his insistence on being in control. The arrogance he displayed with an offer of giving me a one-acre parcel and a house just did not overwhelm me, nor did I actually think he would do anything for me without a huge price tag of betrayal. I was the only heir who could make his life easy, and I simply could not sign over 23 acres without one hell of a fight.

With time on my side while visiting with my mother in Rhode Island, I decided to visit the Town Hall of Bourne, and I spoke with one of the board members, Mr. Brady. I spelled out my position with the land, and mentioned that the developer said his special permit would affect my land. Mr. Brady replied, "That's what he says." He also said I'd better get myself a damned good real estate attorney.

I thanked this board member for his time and information, and left the Bourne Town Hall with the feeling that I was in big trouble, indeed.

My father's probate was in process with my attorney and something inside of me was telling me not to proceed with him.

I was like Little Red Riding Hood, walking on my family woodlot, with the wolf waiting on the other side ready to destroy me.

Later on, after all the years of litigation, everything rang true. My probate attorney and the developer sold the land, with the real estate commissioner, right in the very same office, along with my attorney's partner. Just remember, when you have that gut feeling, you always need to trust your instincts.

Next on my agenda, I had to get back certain papers that I had given this probate attorney, along with abstract papers, to assist me with land court. The most important paper was an original legal document stating everything my father listed in his affidavit to show proof, in a case of adverse possession. This affidavit, signed by my father, was of extreme importance to enter into evidence on an adverse possession case. I filed the affidavit in the Massachusetts court of law.

Finally, I had a day of opportunity open up for me to pay a visit to my probate attorney, while he was not there. I spoke with his secretary and asked to see my legal papers, and she brought them out to me. I proceeded to take the most important papers back into my possession. The secretary got very upset with me as she watched me take my papers from my attorney's file. She said, "You can't do that," and I replied, "They are my papers and I want them."

I told her to calm down, and I dictated a brief letter to her boss, informing him that I no longer needed his services, and that I would be in touch.

Without any hesitation, I needed to find another attorney to handle my father's probate, as that was important and necessary in order for me to establish my father's 10% share of the land, which was willed to me. It would also be necessary to prove adverse possession in court. An old friend in the area guided me to a certain law firm, and I proceeded from there on my father's probate. This friend was a state representative, whom I used to hang out with during high school days.

Come to find out, I could not use this law firm, as I was told by the attorney, himself, that there would be a conflict of interest, because he represented the developer on the golf course side of my family woodlot. There were other legal entanglements, as well, and the partnership with the developer at that time would not consider paying any out-of-pocket expenses, which I was advised to request by a San Diego attorney. I was in a huge trap. No matter which way I turned, there was no way out, except to pray to God and receive from above what my next move would be.

An off-Cape attorney would have been the best choice to make, but a decision was made to go with an attorney my father had used years before, and he was close to home in Buzzards Bay, and had an office in Boston, as well. Mr. Zelman was fatalistic, just like all the other attorneys I dealt with, because everything was pretty well locked up with the wolf developer controlling everything behind closed doors.

After so many years had passed with no legal proceedings held due to a 20-year period necessary for adverse possession, the mail became a source of headaches for me. There were schemes from my relatives pouring out like a mad hornet's nest busting out, stinging me over and over again. It became very clear that my cousin, Peter, who was my Aunt Marjorie's son, became the land organizer who sent letters to other relatives, who were heirs in the 23-acre family woodlot. This was all done prior to my adverse possession case entered into the Massachusetts court of law.

I received a letter from a Hyannis real estate law firm, who wanted all the heirs to deal with a local developer, along with them, for a 50-percent split. This particular law firm out of

Hyannis represented many land developers and did substantial administrative work before the various town boards. Two of the attorneys in their firm were on the Town Council for three different towns on Cape Cod. They would be able to obtain subdivision approval for the parcels in accordance with the Town of Bourne's zoning by-laws.

All of this information was sent from Cousin Peter as Woodlot Information Update 1 on January 10, 1990, and Woodlot Update 2 on May 8, 1990. These update letters were sent out to all the heirs of the woodlot who were involved, so they could get all of this resolved before their time ran out for adverse possession against my father, Richard Curry, and myself.

After I had received their offer to derail me, I decided to call and give this firm a piece of my mind. I listened to his 50 percent scheme with his real estate law firm, who would benefit, and replied with, "They should deal with me instead of my relatives." This attorney started to stutter, and stated that he could not do that. I replied, "No way will I go along with my relatives' wishes, as I work solely on my own."

Then, surprisingly, another registered letter came from Cousin Peter, stating his Hyannis law firm had decided not to go any further with this project, due to the fact that hardly any of the heirs wanted to become involved, and didn't even show up for a requested meeting with the law firm. At the end of his letter, Cousin Peter said that he would not stop there for his mother's share of the land.

The time element for adverse possession is 20 years in the State of Massachusetts, and my greedy relatives only had two years left to try whatever legal strategy they could come up with next. Time was of the essence for all of them.

Since I had no contact with the wolf developer abutting our family property, I would soon pay the consequences with an astounding tax bill that no one could meet, unless you had a lot of money. All of my taxes were paid in full up to 1988, but I had a setback in 1989 due to a sudden recurrence of my mother's cancer, and then losing her to the dreaded disease. I made the decision to quit my job and fly back to Rhode Island, take my mother out of the hospital, under hospice care, to allow her to die at home with dignity.

In 1987, the assessed value of the land was $47,300, and in 1988, the assessed value jumped up to $430,000. The increase was nine times over the previous year of $47,300. This was the beginning of an ongoing pursuit to get rid of me, but little did any of them at the Bourne Town Hall realize my tenacity would prevail for eight years. This greedy developer, who blew down from the Boston area, took hold of the employees of our town hall to set the stage for evil prosperity of old precious historical land in our community of Bourne.

From 1988 through 1990, the assessed taxes remained at $430,000, and then in 1991, the value dropped down to $316,500. At a later date, I was informed that our family woodlot, 23 acres, was land locked. It appeared to me that if all this vacant land was in a land lock status, then someone had terribly miscalculated the assessment of this land to be $430,000.

In October of 1991, I received a Notice of Tax Lien from the Treasurer of Bourne Mr. Coggeshall. I was certainly behind in my taxes, as anyone would be with an assessed value ten times the true value. I spoke with the treasurer about my delinquent taxes, and he told me that if I paid 50 percent of my taxes, I would remain in good standing and he would not foreclose on me. Such action was undertaken, and I sent large amounts of money to this treasurer.

During my conversation with Treasurer Coggeshall, he advised me to call the developer and speak with him. This treasurer chuckled after saying that this particular developer would be the only one, I could deal with, due to the present state of the land. My reply to Mr. Coggeshall was, "Over my dead body."

Needless to say, after those words were given to that treasurer, I declared war on this developer and the Town of Bourne. In 1994, Linda, the new treasurer took over and went forward with land court foreclosure proceedings.

After receiving this upsetting news, I called up my old friend, the State Representative for Bourne, and faxed him all of my cashier's checks, which totaled up to over 50 percent, which was agreed upon with the previous treasurer. In one-and-a-half years, I sent the Town of Bourne over $10,000 in delinquent taxes, which never should have been that high to begin with.

This new treasurer, Linda, soon found out that I was someone who would not be easily pushed around. The State Representative received proper information from the past treasurer's letter requesting 50 percent of the taxes to be paid to make the Town of Bourne happy. I met that critical scenario, and the town wanted to eliminate me like I was some kind of a fly they could just swat. I had an adverse possession case in the court system, along with my Aunt Marjorie's Petition to Partition the land being foreclosed on.

During the time I was drumming up the back tax money, I was basically by myself, and I was literally in a state of, "What am I going to do now?" when I had absolutely nothing. I was a single woman, with no husband or siblings interested in helping me. My father had left me in charge of the land, and jealousy prevailed within my family. I remember sitting out on the patio of my apartment, asking God how I could possibly pay off this large amount of taxes. My heart and soul never felt so much anguish at one time, except for when my

Finally, my prayers were being answered, as God did listen to my cries of desperation to receive money to pay off the taxes. Prior to all my cashier's checks being sent to pay the property taxes, I worked at the East County San Diego Board of Realtors, and worked in several positions for five years. In 1992, I was to encounter my fourth position as the Auditorium Board & Outside Activities Coordinator for the Regency Room, where board functions were held during the week, along with outside activities on weekends, such as wedding receptions, art shows, birthday parties, baptisms, and other various events.

The new Executive Officer for the board made an arrangement with me that if I could bring in $5,000 a month, I would receive a bonus of $250 per month, along with my hourly wage. Previously, I was a real estate agent, and I enjoyed working with people and still held my license, as well. I was quickly given a two-dollar increase in my hourly wage after meeting the arrangement of $5,000 each month for the board on outside functions. This included renting out an extra room upstairs for church equipment, with a year's lease, along with renting the hall each Sunday morning and evening, with one night during the week for their church activities. This was the largest account the board had ever seen, and this all took place after I had my talk with God, crying out to Him and asking for His help to pay those back taxes. It was very interesting that God sent me a steady reliable church group to rent from the board. The minister just blew in like an easy summer breeze, with very little effort on my part at all, as if it was just meant to be.

At this particular time, the board rented a space within the building to TransAmerica, a loan company. I went to a TransAmerica employee that I befriended, explaining my tax dilemma. I was given a $500 loan to start with, and continued on, one loan after the other, with a higher and higher loan amount given each time. They assisted me with all the loans I needed and told me I paid them all off too quickly, and laughed. I was very motivated to receive each monthly bonus, and missed only one in the slow month of January. I was very proud to send all the money necessary on my property taxes. In the end, all my hard work would only be rewarded with more attorney's fees and never-ending taxes.

After sending all those cashier's checks, the treasurer and greedy developer thought, "Why does she keep sending large sums of money?" They were trying very hard to discourage me in every way and I just would not quit. The tax bills continued while the assessed value went down as the town tried to foreclose. It was as if they were setting the stage to lower the value so they could steal the land at a later date.

While time was on my side as the litigation started on my claim with adverse possession, my relatives filed a Petition to Partition the land, and both cases ended up in court together at the same time. The judge needed to decide what to do, and my adverse possession claim proceeded. My father and I had filed back to 1972 for our time frame legally documenting our claim for adverse possession, although with time, my father had over 40 years in his affidavit, and time was of the essence for my relatives to file their petition to divide up the land. The magic year would be up until 1992 for my relatives to file their petition, so they were in a window of time to stop me with all my efforts to keep my promise to my father.

Being a non-resident of Massachusetts and fighting for land clear across country would soon become the massive challenge of my life. On the other hand, I appreciated the fact that the only form of communication from my relatives and the Town of Bourne, working for the greedy developer, with all of their legal maneuvers, was through our postal service. My phone number was unlisted at that time, but their Certified Mail came through loud and clear, sitting and waiting for me in my post office box.

Each time I visited the post office and received the certified paper to pick up from the clerk, all of my insides would shake like a bad car engine. There was always a legal maneuver, and I needed to pray to request God to guide me through the next entanglement with the town officials, my relatives' attorneys, or anything concerning the land, to figure out my next move. This was the chess game of my life, leaving me to figure out what would be the next best move for me in order to win the land. The game was never stacked in my favor, and I always needed to be extra careful to figure out what move to make next.

It was not a nice feeling to be fighting with my relatives, especially when I really held nothing in common with them, except for the genes entering in as a common denominator and that was it. There was no great loss of love because none of us ever visited with each other, except for several cousins who held no interest in this legal taking of the land. These relatives had more of a bond with the developer, the town officials, and their own simple greedy desire to go ahead with the sale of this land.

CHAPTER 10

PRIOR TO COURT PROCEEDINGS

I n the early stages of this eight-year litigation, I realized that everyone was being used in one way or another to serve the wishes of one greedy developer. It was as if I was being pulled in, like movies you see with the poor person who can barely pay their taxes, versus the rich person who is ready to make the quick kill and steal away the most precious personal item you possess.

Once again, the movie is being played, and you are the leading lady trapped in a real life of living hell, with such a powerful force of greed that you just can't quit the film given to you. The promise you made to your father keeps you going, but you never realized just how difficult it was going to be to keep this promise you made.

In 1992, it all started with legal papers flowing in like a whirlwind in an effort to acquire this parcel of land before it was too late for the developer, relatives, and anyone else that would benefit unjustly.

After receiving my Petition to Partition the land document in April of 1992, signed by my Aunt Marjorie, I needed to go back to Massachusetts for a deposition. Almost one year later, in April of 1993, I received a deposition in the mail from my relatives' attorney, Mr. Blackmon. There would be many questions asked of me, and my answers would go on record at a later date in land court.

This deposition was given in April of 1993, in Buzzards Bay, and was held at the office of the attorney for my relatives. Dates and years were entered with information as to who did what when, and how often the relatives visited, and who really cared about the land. The taxes were of prime concern, because at that point, I was behind in taxes, as the appraised value had gone up nine times the assessed value in an effort to squeeze me out. All information was laid out on the table, with no property tax amount ever paid by my relatives.

My Aunt Marjorie gave a deposition, as well, with questions asked of her regarding the family property. I remember her making the statement that her brother, Richard, (my father), was a very sensitive person, and we certainly agreed with that fact. History was what my father lived for. Being sentimental about the Perry history, with land being passed down from one generation to another, was my father's crime, to be so sensitive that, in the end, he asked his daughter to save the land prior to his death. As he traveled around the world in the service as a merchant mariner, he had a gift with his stories being told, with all the particulars of history from each country he was blessed to have encountered.

During my weekly visit to the post office, I received information from my relatives' attorney requesting a Summary Judgment hearing on the land. My own attorney, Mr. Zelman, stated to me over the telephone that it was not necessary for me to be present in court. As a layman, I asked myself, what is a Summary Judgment hearing? I did some research and was connected with a Massachusetts law network, and I discovered that it meant that if Summary Judgment was granted, it would preclude me from taking any further action.

In other words, my relatives and their attorney and developer partner wanted to take the easiest route possible in an effort to speed things up with the land. I figured if that was the situation, it would be wise for me to be present at this hearing, so I would not find myself at a dead-end street, as they desired.

My relatives' attorney cancelled the first date for the Summary Judgment hearing, and I thought the odds were in my favor to show up for the next date scheduled. I was correct and glad, as I needed to travel from California to Boston for this hearing.

When the second date for this Summary Judgment hearing was nearing, I decided nothing would deter me from attending. Arrival time came in May of 1994, with Fiancé Fred and I arriving in Boston with great determination to prevail in this lawsuit.

During a visit with my attorney in Boston, I was told that Mr. Blackmon was going to try to have my father's written affidavit thrown out at this hearing. This was the first time I had heard about this action involving my father's legal affidavit. I really began to wonder about my attorney, and whether he was in cahoots with my relatives' attorney or working for me at this juncture. I was given this information after I presented a written statement to my attorney declaring that I had a right to stand in front of the judge in an effort to explain why I was appearing, and demanded that my attorney allow me to speak with this judge.

After that, I found out that it was a wise choice I had made. My own attorney told me to send my father's original affidavit to him in the mail prior to this meeting, and I said that if the affidavit got lost in the mail, that would be the only proof I had with my father's signature on it. My attorney said that he would inform the court I had sent it, and I told him that would not be good enough in a court of law.

At the time, I worked for a property management company, and my boss advised me to visit one of our escrow companies and have the escrow officer give her seal and verify that the copy sent was from the original affidavit. My attorney appeared angry when I would not send the original, and that made my appearance in Boston a definite asset for me, as I did not trust anyone. I felt that if I did not protect myself, I would not have any future opportunity of any legal venture after that.

I received information from the other side instructing me to play it smart and pay attention to my feelings of foul play. This was a large parcel of land they were attempting to steal from me. I had my armor on for this venture into court and hoped I would have another round of battle before the enemy could take me down.

Upon my arrival at my attorney's office in Boston, I noticed he appeared to be pretty nervous. My relatives' attorney, Mr. Blackmon, had not returned his call to verify he would meet us in court. We waited several hours for a response, and finally, his secretary called two hours prior to hearing time to inform us that he was driving from the Cape to meet us in court.

As we walked from my attorney's office to the courthouse, I reiterated to him my insistence on speaking with this judge at the hearing, and he agreed. I held all of my legal documents in my briefcase and guarded it carefully. If the original affidavit my father had signed was to come into question, I certainly had it in my possession. Needless to say, I was nervous in court and knew that I would be so glad when this was all over.

We met Mr. Blackmon in court, out in the hallway, while we waited for our case to be heard. Fred and I spoke a few cordial words to him, but my attorney, Mr. Zelman, spoke with Mr. Blackmon as if they were two old friends who had just found each other.

The time came to go into court and wait for the judge to make an appearance. The judge entered and was a woman, and I felt comfortable, thinking she might listen to my plea of hardship in my endeavor to keep this precious old land I was fighting for.

From the very beginning, the judge questioned Mr. Blackmon as to why he cancelled his first Summary Judgment hearing date, and he explained to her that another date took precedence over this one. This judge gave me the impression that if he had not attended this hearing date, he would not be in very good standing with her, as her desire to run a tight ship was evident.

The hearing started with Mr. Blackmon stating that there was a case where, if a man was deceased, his affidavit would no longer be acceptable. He proceeded to say that my father's affidavit should be thrown out because he was deceased. The judge spoke up and replied "Well, he can't speak up right now, can he?" She stated that his affidavit was valid and signed, and would not be thrown out.

My attorney, Mr. Zelman, got up and said several things, and asked, what was my father to do to keep my relatives off the land -- stand guard with a gun watching over the land? After that remark, he informed the judge that his client wanted to speak with her. My relatives' attorney, Mr. Blackmon, responded by throwing his arms in the air, and made a facial expression which appeared as a tantrum, just like a child would have when he didn't get his way.

Immediately, the judge asked me to stand and speak, and I very nervously stood up and held my notes and spoke to her. "Your honor, my father and I have been the only two people who have cared about this land, and only when a developer arrived on the scene did all this legal nonsense begin. Yes, I am behind in taxes, but other elements have been working against me in an effort to force me to stand before you today. I want to have my day in court and prove the land belongs to my father and me.

After speaking to the judge, I asked her if she would like to see all of the papers in my briefcase, and she said loudly, "That will be for the courts to decide." I sat down after that statement from the judge. She said a few more things, and we were all out of court within a few minutes.

As Fred and I walked along with my attorney, back to his office, Mr. Zelman said with great enthusiasm, that he felt strongly it would go to trial. Deep inside, my feelings were telling me to get ready for the next round of battle.

Prior to my trial date, I received disturbing news in the form of a letter that said that my attorney, Mr. Zelman, could no longer practice law, as the Massachusetts Bar Association had taken away his right to practice. In the meantime, a new attorney was assigned from the same office building, with the same last name as mine. If I had it to do over again, he would not have been my choice of attorney at all, but I went along due to my location being so far away.

Next on the agenda was the trial I had wished for, to have my day in court, but it was not exactly the best time of year to travel, in the middle of the winter, on February 6, 1995. Needless to say, this date will always be crystal clear in my mind, as Fred and I walked the streets of Boston with a wind chill factor of 30-below.

Furthermore, my flight from San Diego to Boston was cancelled on February 4th due to a snow storm. At the airport, I pleaded the urgency of my situation to the travel agency. I needed to speak with my attorney one day before the trial.

February 6th was my date to appear in court, as that was the date given on the trial docket.

After Fred and I received our new flight, we ended up being stranded in Cincinnati, Ohio, for seven hours, before we could take a small plane to Rhode Island. All the hotels were booked due to the ice-skating tour going on in Rhode Island, so we ended up renting a car and driving out of the city, to a small motel in the country.

The next morning, we drove to the Boston suburb area, where I met my second attorney, Mr. Curry, for the first time, one day before the trial. We spoke over the phone quite a bit, and I wrote him several letters from California including too much detail. He said I was too wordy. If he only knew I was writing about him now, he probably would not be surprised. This attorney was very brief, as he charged a certain amount, so no hourly fee was involved, and I gave him way too much information to contend with.

Unfortunately, I was at a disadvantage not being a Massachusetts resident and having to travel clear across the country, and pay the extra cost of lodging, food, and car rentals. It was not easy.

The loophole was that the developer needed one relative to work with in order to buy out all the rest of the heirs to the land. In order for the deed to be reborn again, certain events needed to occur in the future. The original deed was burnt up in the 1840's fire in Sandwich, where all the records were stored.

Now that I was considered an outsider, traveling from California to address my business issues with the land, the Town of Bourne and I made strange bedfellows. I remember, prior to the trial date, how I felt like an outcast from my home state of Massachusetts. I remember walking into the Town Hall of Bourne and giving my name to the receptionist so I could speak with the treasurer, Linda, and request my tax bill in person, as she would not send the tax bill to me.

I overheard the receptionist speaking with the treasurer, and the girl was giggling and staring at me while I waited. I felt very uncomfortable. Then a man came out and stood in the hallway, staring at me for a long time, and I asked him finally if he would like to take a picture of me. He ran back to whatever office he came from. My name was quite popular in the Town Hall of Bourne, as the designated town officials all worked together against one determined woman fighting for what she believed in.

Another time, I walked into the Town Hall of Bourne and requested to speak with the assessor. I informed them that the past assessor, Mr. Mathison, raised the assessed value ten times the amount that it had been, and I wanted to know why. She admitted that it was not her, and that the previous assessor was no longer there. The present assessor told me my land was landlocked, and that I should speak with the developer who is next to the land. All of the town officials always advised me to speak with the developer.

No one wanted to assist me until I spoke with the State Representative and furnished him with information, including tax payments and the foreclosure notice from the present treasurer, Linda. Tom, my old high school friend, knew I had enough information against the Town of Bourne to sue all of them, if need be. I met the agreement to pay 50 percent of my back taxes, and then some, so the foreclosure did not take place.

CHAPTER 11

BATTLE BEGINS IN COURT

Before the trial began, I decided to meditate in the lady's restroom in an effort to control my nerves before I faced the judge. There was a very old wooden chair I sat on while meditating, and I could feel the old features surrounding me, and I knew this would be a memorable, eventful day. Out in the hallway, there was a sign on a tripod that read, "Curry versus Curry," with a date and time on it. Let this day begin and be over with is what I thought.

My fiancé and I sat in the courtroom waiting for whoever would be appearing. I knew my cousin, John, would be there, but did not realize my Aunt Marjorie, who filed the Petition to Partition, would not be present, or her son, Peter, who initiated this action. My cousin John walked in and looked right at me and nodded, while I looked at him with fire burning in my eyes. This was no social event for me, I was at war fighting for land, with a promise I gave to my father. Dealing with relatives who only cared about their own greed is what really was transpiring. No history in their hearts for our sea-fearing ancestors at all!

There were only two witnesses on my relatives' side, John and his brother, Philip Curry. The horrific weather of Boston either kept the other heirs away, or they were afraid to come and show their faces. Cousin Johnny would be the one who would benefit the most, so it was imperative that he be there in person. Philip was there for moral support, for his brother, and I think, was nosy and wanted his little share of the pie.

When the judge entered the courtroom, I had an anxiety attack, where the nervous system was way out of control. Having to endure courtroom drama in a fight against your relatives was not exactly my cup of tea, but I needed to be present to continue with my promise.

My attorney, Mr. Curry, told me it was time for me to get up and give my testimony in front of the judge. I felt sick to my stomach while I was sitting, but as soon as I stood up, miraculously, I felt completely calm inside. Spirit had come through for me, as I had requested assistance so that I wouldn't be so nervous in front of the judge this time.

My actions and appearance, along with my words, were very important in front of this judge, in order for him to know I was a credible and honest person. I chose to act not only for myself, but for my father, who could not be present in the human flesh, but only on paper, as the sworn affidavit he had signed was as good as it could be in this court of law.

Both attorneys asked questions, and of course I felt more comfortable when my attorney asked questions. Then my relatives' attorney cross-examined me. I needed to be very careful to give the correct answers while the judge listened intently. This was no ordinary day, as I finally was having my day in court. Persistence paid off, and I thanked God I had my best foot forward, and was grateful I was not acting in a disjointed, nervous state, but conducting myself in a professional manner.

There was another sworn affidavit that my friends, Sue and Alan, had signed, which stated many of the things I had done concerning the land and what they both witnessed, but neither of them felt it was important enough to appear in court. Alan told me that my attorney told him he did not need to be present, and then my attorney told me it was critical for them to be there. So, who lied to me?

Prior to the trial, my girlfriend, Sue, called me in California and said that her husband had a hernia operation scheduled on the same date as the trial. The operation could have been rescheduled, but of their free-will, they chose to stick with that date in an effort to escape the requested court appearance, which would have meant the world to me. This upset me, as no true friend would do such a thing, when I had asked for their help.

After receiving this depressing news from my friend, I went and cried silently as I sat in a bath. My fiancé knocked on our bathroom door and asked if I was all right, and I lied and said, "Yes," but he knew how disappointed I was.

Later when the trial was over, we visited my brother, Jeoffrey, at his house in Rhode Island. My friends lived in the same state, and usually we would go out to dinner together at a special seafood restaurant whenever I visited Rhode Island. This time was different due to their lack of interest appearing at my trial. I invited them over to my brother's house for dinner. They wanted to know why we didn't have dinner at our favorite seafood restaurant. Sue and Al could not wait to tell us they had just purchased land in New Hampshire, and my fiancé let them have it. "You chose not to be there for Sandra, even though your appearance, as well as your affidavit, was needed at the trial." They got up and left and I knew I most likely would not see them again, and I felt agony in my heart.

Another disappointment came when I asked my mother's

sister, Barbara, to be a witness at trial, as she was still alive. My grandfather, Paradise, owned the land right next to the woodlot. My Aunt Barbara dated my father first, and then he met my mother, after their meeting as young kids, with my dad on his Harley. My Aunt Barbara could have verified everything written on my father's affidavit, but she chose not to. Yes, another affidavit could have been written, but my Aunt Barbara said that she needed a wheelchair and could not walk that well, so there was another valid witness who would not show up in person for the trial. I never held that against her, but I thought to myself, it was not meant to be. I remember her telling me I carried all of this for too many years with this land. So, I wondered if she knew how much it tormented me, why not help me? There was a lot of jealousy between my mother and her sister, I believe.

During my testimony, I felt quite confident that I was handling the cross-examination from Mr. Blackmon, who tried to trip me up with an exact property location on a map. As a young child, I walked that property with my father, and he showed me the exact location of the property boundaries, with his knowledge as a town surveyor. There was a large map, and the attorney requested that I put an X on a certain location on the property, and it was entered into the record as an exhibit.

Next, my cousin, John, got up to testify, and his attorney questioned him about a certain location, as well, and he did not appear to know the exact location. I thought, if Mr. Blackmon wanted to make me look stupid, his client did not appear to be any better informed than I was. I did not think this was a crucial point in the case, but my relatives' attorney made a big scenario regarding this certain location on the land. I had posted "No Trespassing" signs and "No Hunting" signs, along with pictures of myself in different years and locations on the property. All the signs posted were definitely on the property in question. When it came to pointing to a definite location on a map, then I was no expert, other than what my father had pointed out during our walks.

Twenty- three acres is a large parcel of land, and there were over three acres of swamp land, along with the humidity, which created a lot of mosquitoes during the summertime. It is doubtful that my relatives had their family picnics there, as they stated in an effort to prove they used the property. This was so far-fetched, as anyone who knows the Cape would agree, to gather together on undeveloped land at that time of the year.

While John testified that he cut wood, along with another cousin, Alan, who chose not to appear in court, he did not mention where the proper location was to cut wood. In October of 1986, I met briefly with the developer on his property, and he said that both of my cousins had cleared wood off of his parcel of land by mistake, because they did not know the exact boundaries, and he laughed about it.

During the trial, I was stunned to learn that my Aunt Eleanor Gardner had expired, and also my cousin Peter, who had initiated the newsletters to everyone. Aunt Eleanor had been in a nursing home for years, but Peter was fairly young and died of a heart attack. Aunt Eleanor left her son David in charge of her estate, and he did not hesitate to accept his percentage from his mother. My cousin Alan, grandson of Eleanor, chose not to appear in court against me, as he felt his Uncle Dick (my father) was the only heir who truly loved the history involved in our family land.

The new player had to be my cousin John, due to the fact that Peter died, and my Aunt Marjorie was in her 80s, and no longer had a great deal of interest in this trial like she once did.

Therefore, everything made sense, as the developer needed a

new heir to manipulate, to try to keep the Petition to Partition going to acquire the land, with John acting as the new leader of the pack. He fell into a default situation where he could now play cards with the cunning wolf and have his very own backroom deal.

Amazingly, there were only three witnesses at the trial, and I am sure my cousin Peter, if he were alive, would have been center stage, not cousin Johnny. I had two cousins present now, John and his brother, Philip Curry, against me in court. It was actually funny how all the other relatives had no desire to be there. Who do you think would really profit at the end of all this legal mess? John, would find out, at a much later date, who he was dealing with, firsthand.

After my sworn testimony, John, his brother, Philip, and I made our departure from the courtroom. I was relieved to have this trial behind me and chose not to speak with my cousins. Fred and I picked up our coats and went in a different direction from my cousins so I would not be tempted to act irrationally.

In the end, Philip's testimony was thrown out, as his remarks were just hearsay so John was the only one against me in court. Needless to say, the decision from the judge would take forever to receive, and the waiting game was on.

While Fred and I waited for the decision from the judge, I prayed for all of this to be over so that I could get on with a normal way of life.

Unfortunately, I received the decision through the mail, and I shall never forget that day. After waiting from February 6, 1995, to July 3, 1995, I received more mentally disturbing news in my post office box, as the judge did not rule in my favor. As far as the adverse possession claim, my father and I had failed to demonstrate that our use was exclusive, continuous, and uninterrupted for a period of 20 years.

Regarding my alternative claim for contribution for payment of taxes on the property, and damages, including interest, costs, and reasonable attorney's fees, the judge ruled in my favor. The only thing would be reimbursement for back property taxes paid since 1963, and legal interest accrued, jointly and severally, by the defendants. The reasonable attorney's fees did not ring true, except for future fees, as a very small percentage would only apply in the event of an upcoming appeal after this decision from the trial.

If my father and I had installed a fence around this large parcel of land and grown tomatoes or been living on the land every year, we would have been in a much better position to claim possession. My relatives only had hearsay as to what they claim they did, and my father was the only heir to the land to step forward and prove his ancestry, and pay the years of back taxes. Taxes alone were not good enough, and in reality, my father had used the property since he was 16 years old, when he first met my mother. Prior to my father's departure from the Cape in 1978, when he came to live in California, until his death in 1986, my father had used that land for over 40 years.

I was not ready to give up quite yet and decided to file for an appeal. Why not at least try all of my options, I thought to myself? So, on it goes with another round of fighting.

CHAPTER 12

THE APPEAL AND AUCTION ON LAND

After suffering defeat with the trial, I decided to file an appeal. A different attorney should have been sought out, and the fact that I didn't do that would turn out to be a terrible decision on my part, which I had to live with as well as the realization, that my two attorneys were not working in my best interest. Little did I know that my second attorney would annoy me immensely. All he cared about was that another $2,500 would be given to him to present my appeal. I remember my second attorney, and not by my selection, Mr. Curry, (no relative) mentioning that he had lived in Monument Beach several years prior, when he had a summer cottage there. I never realized, until it was too late, that he cared more about the employees in the Town of Bourne than his own client.

However, I could not quit now. It was on to the next battle. I knew I could not stop until I had exhausted everything, I had in me.

During the time of this upcoming appeal, I took it upon

myself to seek out some cases pertaining to adverse possession at the San Diego Law Library. I was guided to several cases in Massachusetts, and I sent them to my attorney, but he would not discuss them with me, as I was just a layman. But I was the person with the most to lose, and I wanted to understand the laws of the state the land was in, to be of assistance. I did not pay him by the hour, and I realized he did not want to give me the time of day to discuss, basically, anything at all. The very bare minimum is all I received. And in the end, I never even knew the date the appeal was to be presented. It was only when the appeal was over that I found out the ruling was not in my favor.

I received the appeal ruling dated 11-25-97, with Ruling 1.28, and a letter from the attorney in which he said that it was self-explanatory. He never even gave me a copy of the brief he submitted to the appellate court prior to the appeal date. That did not sit well with me, as he was my legal counsel, and I realized he did not act in my best interest.

Needless to say, my association with Mr. Curry turned sour when he breached his attorney-client duty to communicate his actions with me.

Next, I requested a copy of the brief given by my attorney to the appeals court, and I had to threaten to seek out the Board of Overseers in Boston if he declined my request.

A copy was sent, after I had already paid for a copy from the appellate court, as I could not wait any longer for my attorney to do what he was supposed to do. It appeared that no matter what path I took, I had obstacles thrown at me, and that included my own attorneys, who appeared to be sleeping with the enemy.

Upon termination of my second attorney, I hired a third attorney from the Mid Cape area, who I believed would not be in cahoots with all the players in Bourne. My second attorney was upset with me, and he would not send my new attorney, Mr. Perrino, any of my legal paperwork. If he did not want to work with me, then why not do the normal formalities and send all of my paperwork to this new attorney? I mentioned to my past attorney that I would go to the Town of Bourne, myself, and discuss all the unfair things that were going on, and he told my fiancé, Fred, not to allow me to go and speak with any town officials. A red flag went up. I had every right to speak my mind and ask questions, as I was the only heir paying taxes on this land.

Therefore, my third attorney Mr. Perrino was put in place for whatever would transpire next in this no-win situation I found myself in. I received a Certified Letter from a woman attorney who had represented me during my father's probate. She was now representing my Cousin, John Curry. She sent me an offer to sell the property, with Cousin John representing all the other heirs. The offer sent to me was very low, while the appraised amount was much higher. Remember, there was no clear deed to this land, so an heir to the property needed to sell it and distribute the proper percentages to the other heirs.

Meanwhile, I had been in contact with an interested party several years prior, who owned a parcel of land adjoining our land. We kept in touch with each other throughout the years and formed an alliance. The access problem could be worked out for both sides, and that was the interest we shared. Mr. Bertowski was a retired developer, and we shared information and contacted my third attorney for our next move.

The town had me in a land-lock status, and I had no assistance from anyone to make it otherwise. With that type of status, other interested parties would be null and void. Without any legal access, no one else could possibly make an offer, except for Mr. Bertowski.

This secret player on my side would soon enter the arena and find out for himself, firsthand, what I had been going through for many years. The greedy town officials were, once again, in partnership with this wolf developer, working together to finish me off for good, thereby ending this eight-year-long litigation.

A higher offer was not accepted by the acting real estate commissioner involved in the sale of the land. My new partner contacted his attorney and my third attorney to establish a date in court, in front of a judge, to allow a higher offer to be entered and put on the table.

Presenting a higher offer, would give more money to all of my relatives, who would receive their percentages. Cousin John didn't receive much money from his share of the land, but he was in it for the grand prize in the backroom, bidding for the cunning wolf.

The date was set and the judge asked my attorney what he thought. Mr. Bertowski told me that my attorney didn't fight hard enough for me. On the other hand, Mr. Bertowski's attorney fought very hard for this higher offer to be accepted, so I was very grateful for that.

Just imagine all the dirty tricks I needed to go through, and they thought I was finally boxed in, with no way to get out. I could strike out one more time to make them stay inside the law, with assistance, of course, from Mr. Bertowski.

Once again, I needed to pay an attorney to go to court, and my third attorney was $200 an hour. We worked out my fees to be paid after the sale of the land. My partner was a pretty tough cookie, and his attorney was no one to be pushed around. I needed someone like him to be my attorney from the very beginning of all this legal mess.

The judge decided to allow bidding to take place on the property, where Mr. Bertowski would meet with John Curry and bid on the land. My cousin's attorney had mentioned in court that John had mortgaged his house for the property, and the judge was not too impressed with that.

Finally, a date was given, and the real estate commissioner started a bidding war, which was to take place between Cousin John and Mr. Bertowski, at the law office of Ford O'Connor, on MacArthur Blvd. This office is where it all started with my very first attorney (deceased now), who advised me to speak with the developer. A full circle of greed had been completed with a confirmation of my accurate feelings all along!

The final act, I thought at that time, came and the bidding began, but my Cousin John was not alone in the room, as my silent partner Mr. Bertowski received a huge surprise with the appearance of the greedy developer. My attorney had not given him that information, and he was not very happy with that type of a bomb.

During the bidding, the developer nodded his head each time to my cousin for him to make a higher bid, showing his true colors of greed with the man who would do anything to acquire what was never his and showed no act of common decency.

Unfortunately, Mr. Bertowski did not have enough money to outbid the developer who continued to nod his head each time a higher bid was given, as Cousin John acted as a puppet to do the dirty bidding for him. With a higher offer from Mr. Bertowski, the bidding went up $80,000 more for the developer to pay. There was some small satisfaction out of this higher offer, just to see him squirm and show just how low a snake he really was. I knew it all along in my soul who I was dealing with, from the very beginning.

How could anyone go and hold their head high, walking through the Town of Bourne, having full knowledge of all the dirt he carried within? This rings true for my Cousin John and his partner in crime, the developer, and in the end, I heard that my cousin had a lawsuit against his partner, who used him for his own gain. How could this be?

After the bidding was over, Mr. Bertowski walked over to the developer and said, "You'd better get yourself a much larger bed, as your bed is too damn small with all the town people in bed with you."

Therefore, I may enlighten you now about how happy I am to have finished this chapter explaining the major legal aspects of the land, so my soul may finally heal, as part of me has felt dead inside. My inner soul may start the healing process as I write these last few words on this past litigation.

With time on my side, I may finally find healing, because each time I would sit down to write, I needed to face my demons. It has taken many years to pull up all the emotions and put them on paper to explain what really happened along my spiritual journey of hell. Time was the healing force for me to be able to release this bad energy. It was as if I were poisoned, and it has taken all these years to work out, along with my special gift of writing, to tell each and every one of you my whole true story from within my heart and soul. The difficult part is over, and now I will be able to work on the spiritual chapters for the rest of my book. I will be guided to write with my extraordinary gift God has bestowed upon me through my automatic writing.

CHAPTER 13

WISDOM FROM ABOVE

Throughout my studies at my church from September 1985 to July 1995, I prepared for my departure from my minister and church members. At that time, I didn't know that was the time frame known as my "spiritual graduation." I was to be advanced with a spiritual gift in such a way that my life would have a new twist of meaning.

Everything I learned was through my own determination to acquire and understand what it was like on the other side, and why certain elements on the spiritual side had such an impact on my life. The crossing over of someone so dear to me, so precious, created a need to know more. I was unaware as I was being drawn into this spiritual side, that it was really where I should be. My direction in life was right on track, and due to the powerful love connection, I had with my father.

In February of 1995, after going back east to Massachusetts for a trial against my relatives over land, my life would change yet again, as one door would close while another door would soon open.

While I was waiting for a decision from the Massachusetts judge, a new beginning was about to unfold, one that I could not have foreseen. A certain amount of misery would surface, where the past needed to rear its ugly head and start to make some kind of sense of things to come. While everything was not quite worked out, events were in the making for a new style of life, one that would emerge from the ashes.

During our weekly meditation at church, I received the most beautiful healing, even though my world was filled with uncertainty. A tumor was discovered in my breast, and I lost the trial over the land, so I was at the lowest of lows. While meditating, a huge Kelly-green cross appeared, with a pitch-black background, symbolizing my particular stage of darkness, where my life would turn around for the better with a divine healing from above.

Faith restored my soul after a miraculous healing, combined with three healings in one; 1) no cancer was found after removing my lump; 2) there was no need for medication; and 3) (the greatest of all) receiving my automatic writing gift through spirit. Yes, the precious sign of the cross in the healing color of Kelly-green was given during my meditation, representing to me that the Father, the Son, and the Holy Spirit were there for me at my darkest hour. Oh, the joy of it all!

I was off in my new direction with my new gift. My spiritual church had served its purpose for ten years, and I no longer needed my minister to teach me. I would be able to communicate with my father through spirit now, all on my own.

Beyond this new gift was a new awareness for me, as I was able to ask questions and receive answers from the other side with no third-party connection through my minister. I was the new spiritual channel or medium that meditated and sought out knowledge, as needed at that given time, to provide wisdom from above.

As time went on, it was given to me that when I asked for answers to certain questions, Spirit wanted me to call it "Wisdom from Above" and date it. My e-mail address, "Wisdom Above," derived from my early beginnings with this spiritual gift of automatic writing.

To acquire the rare gift of automatic writing gave me a sense of purpose, to know that I would be able to assist all types of people who desire someone to guide them on their path. In my quest to write "*Your Soul's History*," my gift has assisted me with spelling out my journey in words, and has enabled me to express to all my readers how possible everything is in life. For me to be able to give readings to those who want to understand spiritualism, and how Spirit works within all of us, and share this uniqueness from the other side, gives me great inner peace.

This ongoing gift became my new best friend, and whenever I required answers, I would simply go within and meditate. Through this new awareness, I derived a sense of inner peace and understanding that there was a true and higher awareness just waiting for me, and all I needed to do was meditate to be able to enjoy the gift.

As I continue to write and explain the many spiritual path's we all need to travel, I find that many of us are weary travelers on this earth plane of ours. Also, that the true meaning of life has a setting, much like they use in a movie to set the stage. We find ourselves as individuals walking here on earth, creating our own unique movie sets for where we choose to be. Our paths could be changed at any given moment, with just a blink of an eye, just as a movie script changes constantly. Interestingly enough, when we all reach the other side, we watch the movie of our lifetime on the earth plane, and it is imperative you watch the leading actor or actress – yourself.

What does that mean for most of us, who all of a sudden may need to go within and ask, "Why now?" Some of the questions we carry within us as we travel through life are answered in some fashion or another, and we may not understand at that time, but later on, down the road, it makes sense, when we are not seeking the answers.

There are other times when we simply just don't get it at all, as the meaning is just not clear to see, smell, or touch. That is very normal, as we humans will never understand all the answers we have, while we say to ourselves, "Why now, dear Lord?"

So, what is the big question we all have in common: Why are we all here on this earth plane of ours? The answer is that we all need to experience our spiritual lesson on earth. During our brief visit on earth, we experience what is the only way to acquire spiritual growth, or to learn our spiritual lesson. You may choose earth, or several other planets, in order to advance yourself spiritually. To acquire your spiritual growth and reach a passing grade on earth is the easiest way to receive self-attainment. You may not advance in quite the same fashion remaining in heaven where there is all good and no evil. There is a balancing act on earth. Within yourself, you need to perform good or evil acts, as everyone has free will to do as they choose, in order to reach their spiritual lesson, whatever lesson that may be. Reincarnation comes into play, as there are many mansions in heaven and as you seek higher perfection with God on earth, the closer you are to remain in the kingdom of heaven forever.

What have we established here with the knowledge of our spiritual lesson? The majority of us have no clue regarding the spiritual lesson we all must participate in, whether we know it exists or not. Those people who want to know what it is are actually here to learn within their souls to ask and seek the true information for their own benefit and peace of mind.

Granted, there will be some who won't be too thrilled to learn what their lesson is. Bear in mind that if you are a true seeker of the light, you will want to know, one way or the other, what it is. Some people will say they don't care to know, and in that respect, won't have the true understanding of where they will end up on the spiritual scoreboard when they reach the other side. Believe me, when you go home with God again, you will hope you took the time to know whatever your lesson was, as you may repeat that lesson over and over until you get it right.

Now we shall go right to the heart of things and try to understand why we are here, and have an explanation that will only relate to that individual who receives the lesson. The lesson will hit home, right to their very soul, whatever the spiritual lesson is. As the spiritual lesson unfolds, you will search for a deeper understanding as to why it is imperative for you to complete your lesson, so that you may never repeat that particular lesson ever again. You will need a passing grade in school, just as you are required to attain a good grade with your spiritual lesson, as well. Only when you reach the other side will you see where God will grade you while you were on the earth plane, as you will elevate up or down the various thousands of levels where you will make your new home, so to speak.

Whatever area you are placed in will determine your status while you have your brief visit with God. What, exactly, does that mean? According to your spiritual growth, that is how high up the ladder you shall be. Depending upon your spiritual merit, you will be given a higher or lower rank, and the higher up you are on a spiritual scale, the more privileges you shall be given. On the earth plane, you select your path which guides you to your next level and if you choose wisely, heaven will be more appealing when your life is over.

Therefore, you simply may not escape the true facts of your soul when you go home to the kingdom of God. The truth shall set you free or the truth will tell on you. You do not make it up very high for the simple fact that your soul will make you pay for whatever bad deeds you did on earth. You may have been a corrupt greedy person, who acquired wealth through taking advantage of those who could not fight back, as you stole from others and took their pride and dignity away. The true facts will not serve you well when you reach the other side. Pay-back time will be like tough-love parents give their children, so they will learn of the harshness in life they will experience as they grow up.

Let's hope, for the sake of your soul, that you were not that greedy person, but rather a spiritual person who tried not to step on anyone's toes, and just wanted to be treated in a fair fashion. We all have our own free will to do whatever suits our fancy at the time. Whatever choices you make on your spiritual path here on earth will always be noted on the record sheet one lifetime after another.

Yes, I am an avid believer, in reincarnation, understanding truly that God is a very loving and forgiving God who gives many chances for all our souls to progress. Life on earth is not exactly everything you want. All people experience events such as births, deaths, accidents, marriages, divorces, illnesses, and many other things that come into play throughout our stage of life on earth. Many other people are truly blessed with great fortune, fame and wealth, and do not necessarily enjoy it as much as you might think. Some of these blessed souls would prefer a little less money and an easier way of life, with no publicity. No one is truly happy about everything, or why would they be here, as a spiritual lesson is always necessary when you dwell on this globe.

Each lifetime, we all come down to complete a spiritual lesson, as it is needed, whether we accomplish this particular lesson now or in the future. What that means is that if we fail on this lesson, we are allowed to repeat it over and over again until we complete that particular lesson with a satisfactory grade. Then we go to the next spiritual lesson in another lifetime, and we may only need to experience this lesson once. Depending upon the spiritual lesson, and how difficult it is, it may be necessary for one person not to pass as their soul is not ready yet to complete that lesson to learn. It all depends upon that individual's soul, and how their lesson suits them, according to their own free will on this to advance or not.

As our lessons progress, then we may seek more difficult spiritual lessons, and we might decide to meet with various souls from the past who could assist an individual to conquer the most complicated lesson. We all contribute to and guide others, when they may not be able to go on without encouragement to fight darkness in their life.

If you think you may reach heaven after being here on the earth in just one lifetime, you'd better think again, because in order to remain in heaven with our creator, God, we need to reach perfection first. Why do you think we are given so many chances to acquire our spiritual lessons on earth? We are not perfect to begin with, but with a lot of time and experience under our belts, we may proceed again and again with endless opportunities to reach that perfection we all need. After reaching the ultimate perfection, it is no longer necessary to come down to earth and experience another spiritual lesson, or acquire a human body as a vessel to suffer and die. Our soul may remain in heaven to stay with God eternally, where we started from. When all our reincarnation lessons reach a passing grade as the students we are, then and only then will our soul take a path in the right direction.

Sometimes we wonder why we meet certain people in our lives during different time intervals, and ask ourselves why we have an instant like or dislike of these new souls thrown in our paths. Some of these new characters play an important role, and are given to us so we can figure out what the next turn should be in our lives. It's as if life is one huge puzzle, and we need to put all the thousands of pieces together to try and place the picture in the right perspective.

As time goes by with the tick of the clock, we shall realize we all come closer to being on the other side. We are here on the earth plane for just a brief visit. There are those who would sell their souls if they could live another ten to fifty or more years.

Death is a process you may not change or cheat. You are a human body your very own private vessel. Most people don't think of their bodies as vessels. They think of cars, buses, trains, planes, or ships as our transportation here, but it is our human, God-given bodies that get us from Point A to Point B.

On the other side, you lose your body, as your soul is the only requirement. The growth of your soul determines your progress and where your station shall be. In some cases, with your soul, you may lose a higher position by not attaining what you really could have, due to your free will going to the dark side. If your soul was very good on earth, the higher up your level shall be. This is the time when payback is a true living hell, with side effects for bad conduct such as murder, hatred, greed, along with unprovoked acts of violence toward others.

For those who have lost loved ones due to a disease like cancer, it takes time for the ones left behind to comprehend why there had to be so much suffering. We all come on this globe expecting so much hope, faith, and love, and all of a sudden, a time element appears and takes you to the other side. But please understand that the disease which caused all the suffering was a tool used to take that individual home with God. That individual will never suffer again, as a lesson was applied, and we all have different ailments because we are in the human form with no perfection.

Some people suffer, in one form or another, when they are very young, and may even come close to death, and then they recover and go on to live long and healthy lives. Others make their exit from earth by car accident, on trains, planes, in fires, or shootings and other violent acts.

Always remember that our souls are the continuous pieces of thread that go on and on, not the human body, as the body must eventually die. Each time we come back to experience our spiritual advancement, our soul is there; only the exterior human suit God has chosen for us has changed.

During my transition time of studying spiritualism, I found that trying to understand too much at once about the other side may be overwhelming, as it takes time to absorb things and make sense out of them. With time, I understood more, because I was the type of person who wanted answers to all of my questions.

After ten years of constant learning, I acquired several gifts. The most fascinating thing I found out was that I was right on track for finding myself, and rediscovering different things through past lives, which connected the dots for the here and now. Understanding the past made my awareness as bright as the heavenly lights, and I knew I was walking my path in the direction God wanted me to follow.

It was given to me from Spirit that I would write a book and become a spiritual author for God, and I would assist many people in understanding more about the simplicity of spiritualism. I played an important role long ago and was told of my past associations, which truly inspired my soul to go forward with my automatic writing gift. As I am here now writing, I truly believe the wisdom I receive from above will carry on and go somewhere, as I am writing on a scale I never knew before this gift was bestowed upon me.

As a young child in the fourth grade, my English teacher awarded extra credit to students who wanted to increase their grade. My teacher wanted her students to learn to become creative. She gave us a picture with 15 to 20 words underneath to write a story. That year, I wrote 200 stories, and my grade was already an A, and my teacher said very clearly that I should become a writer. They used to call me the deep thinker as a young child, because I would be all by myself, daydreaming, and my mind would go to other places.

Some of us carry certain traits, characteristics, talents inside for years, and finally one day, the light comes on, with all the brilliance from above, to reveal those special blessings we possessed all along. As for myself, I have realized, through my long lesson of patience, God has given me this talent, along with what they call, in the spiritual world, automatic writing through *Spirit*. What that means is, you possess the gift of writing, but you have assistance from *Spirit* to write what God wants you to write. This automatic writing is a rare gift from God, so when you are blessed with it, your whole life takes on new meaning.

Now you are a spiritual channel. God is able to come through you and teach other people who choose to read a true story, about spiritual awareness. How could anyone not want to write when you can go back in time, filled with energy, and put your thoughts on paper to excite your soul with adventure all over again?

Therefore, as an older adult, you realize you need to go on and write. You can never stop writing when you are able to reach so many souls with a true story of spiritualism, using your rare gift from God to guide you from one chapter to another, sharing what you have already learned.

So here I am, just waiting to entertain you with the truth, as I know it has changed my whole life, personally, with new understanding as to why we are all here and what the spiritual world represents when we all go to the other side. The big question most people want an answer to is, what is on the other side? Know that there is nothing but love surrounding us, as we follow the white light back to our originating home with God.

CHAPTER 14

NEW SPIRITUAL LIGHT

From the very beginning to the very end of this long spiritual journey of mine, I have seen the light when there was barely any light at all, which was during the transitional period of hell on earth for me. When there appears to be no way out of a particular situation revolving around your being, is when you are really put to the test of your faith in God.

During your transit you pray for guidance from above to receive whatever is necessary to keep yourself on the path and to retain your sanity. Your experiences give you more stamina to stick it out and hang tough with your convictions. Each and every day you ride the wheel of life going round and round and there seems to be no end to all of it.

One test after another is so compelling that you continue asking more questions. Why do I need to do this, dear Lord? Why don't I have the answers laid out in front of me?

This life is just too difficult for me. Please make things better for me, you plead, instead of wondering and fighting all the time, with no end in sight of this very long dark tunnel where there is no light at all.

Within time, you keep going due to your great faith in God and at the end of all of your hardships and great endeavors to figure which way to go, you start viewing the bright light at the end of your long spiritual journey to sanity once more.

I remember my minister telling me, "You can't always get what you want." During that moment I thought to myself that was a cruel thing to tell me, but in the end, it was a reality check. At that time, I was in the middle of litigation and keeping my promise to my father, so how could I simply quit? Yes, I had many roadblocks to contend with and each time I requested assistance to go on and I got exactly that. Information was received to continue on and fight again and again until I could no longer carry the cross I needed to bear.

After I was land-locked by the town, so no other developer could enter a bid against the opposing developer, and my cousin Johnny to sell the land through the real estate commissioner, was when the greed came out in full force. I witnessed the powerful grand cycle of evil and corruption as they acquired this old family land, stolen land to line the pockets of yet another greedy developer.

Even the older retired developer I worked with who owned land close to my family property, who addressed the sale of the land at the Rotary in Bourne, could not outbid the wolf developer.

During the sale my cousin was present with the real estate commissioner along with the developer, who nodded his head to my cousin Johnny giving his approval every time the price of the land went higher and higher against Mr. Bertoski.

With no clear title to the land through an heir was the only way for this developer to be successful. At the very beginning the developer stated to me he would give me an acre of land and build a house after the sale of 23 acres was completed. I did not accept his offer due to following my gut feeling; he was not a man of honor or any decency.

Information was given to me that my cousin Johnny was in partnership with the developer and they incorporated the land. They built several homes and were having difficulty selling the last couple of acres due to the location. Whether or not he is happy now, only he knows how he feels deep in his soul. As the old saying goes "Birds of a feather flock together" and I certainly chose not to fly in their flock. Now I am the rare bird left in peace to fly away from both of them forever.

Life goes on, and in the end, you ask, what is next? For me I have found new life with my automatic writing gift through *Spirit*. I have been able to release all of the bad energy I have carried for many years, to reach out to each of you through my writing in *"Your Soul's History."*

To be able to write through this new found gift bestowed upon me, has healed my soul in such a way that this book needed to be shared with all, to tell that there is a new spiritual light at the end of my tunnel, and anyone else's who has great faith in God.

We all need to work hard to acquire our spiritual growth. Just like anything in life that you need to practice—meditation, singing, writing, painting, playing the piano, tennis--golf needs to be practiced to reach a level of satisfaction.

When you reach that level, grasp the brass ring of life to claim your God given gift and the glory of living and breathing on this Earth-plane of ours, combined with the Spiritual world above. That is the ultimate!

We are all strong when we ask God to guide us and give us the wisdom from our Almighty Father. As my ancestors, the Perrys, traveled across the oceans to a better land of opportunity to be able to believe in God, and not be persecuted in such a way is where it all began. In worshipping God and forever following his guidance, we have all prevailed from one century after another. Time does not fall short of our faith and need to remain steadfast in our God-fearing ways and teach our children the precious history throughout various time frames. Our great faith in God will help us to always prevail over evil on this earth plane of ours.

Meantime, I am relieved to be where I am in life right now, so I may share this book. I needed to write this to release hate I held in my heart against those I fought due to my promise to and great love for my father. I realized I lost the land due to tremendous greed taking over, but to be given a gift straight from God, to be able to write of this fatalistic endeavor, has renewed my soul.

Futuristically, I now pray for individuals to seek me out, so I may continue on writing more for all of you again. My next book will no longer include my past, but will reveal what I am really here to do on the earth plane. The past is behind me now and a new beginning before me to utilize the gift of automatic writing given to me from above our Almighty Father in heaven.

CHAPTER 15

THE FINAL ENDING

I now understand that in the end the true reward given to me is to simply write about my experiences. It was not meant to be for me to live on Cape Cod, where my family history was embedded. Living there would not have brought true happiness, only resentment from relatives and other key players.

At the end of this eight-year litigation I found reality creeping in. The entire final outcome was the result of pure greed on the part of others. The process of dealing with a villainous developer, relatives, attorneys and town officials left a very bad taste in my mouth. It was all too much to swallow. Thanks to Dolores Cannon, a wise woman who gave me guidance, this chapter has been added to give you more details.

I omitted the ending in the first draft because I was so devastated with the decision from the court and my dealings with the town I was raised in. Originally, I did not communicate how much this disturbed me. I am writing about this now, so you can feel the details as they affected me during these trials of my faith.

If I took the simple route to deal with the developer abutting my family land, things would have ended differently. I chose the most difficult path with the belief that there was fairness. I made a promise to my father out of great love for him. The history of our seafaring ancestors the "Perrys" was highly important in creating the promise. One could not go without the other. The promise was for me to continue to fight for our family property that had been in the seafaring name of the Perrys from one generation to another since the early 1600's. Their name remains in our U.S. History books today. That part of history will never be taken away like the land was!

For me there was no other choice to make and the journey began with the cards stacked against me. I started out playing a fair and decent game, and soon I became more adept at making my next moves. I became a fast learner due to illegal activities thrown at me from all directions. When my enemies found I could keep my head above water, they were forced to build roadblocks to deter me.

There was no turning back once I started and I prayed for wisdom to keep me on the right track. My good intentions dissolved after realizing the futility of my efforts. The higher force kept me in this fight to teach me that evil does exist in this world.

When you are backed into a corner you usually come out fighting for your life, beliefs, values, integrity with all your strength and grit. You find out who you really are. I discovered great faith, inner strength and the tenacity to face each successive test.

Meditating assisted me with guidance from above to apply the wisdom given to continue. Each time I needed answers I would go within and ask God to guide me. I felt like David going into battle with Goliath. Even David had family who were jealous of his great faith to fight such a giant man. But everything has a reason, and for many years I was tormented with the negative outcome. The heartache and unscrupulous dealings brought me close to having a nervous breakdown.

Yet, I would do it all over again if I needed to. I like the person I have become. The reason is clear and simple for me. I can walk with my head held high knowing I chose good over evil. There is no need for me to go back and change anything I did. Sometimes the ending is not the way you envisioned it and you need to grow and learn and accept the things you cannot change. I have no regrets.

As given in previous chapters there were two cases entered into the court system in Massachusetts. The Adverse Possession Case was not won by me and my father against other heirs of the land. The 20 years my father and I paid on taxes and another 10 years of taxes I paid, along with 40 years of cutting wood and posting signs proved not to be enough. If my father and I had planted a crop of tomatoes or built a fence around the 23 acre-parcel, that may have established a stronger adverse move for possession. Several witnesses at the trial would have added more to the case, if they would have appeared when requested.

Ruled in my favor by the judge, were all the back taxes my father and I paid to the town. Interest would be included for 30 years with reasonable attorney fees. I received all the back tax money and the interest, but no reasonable attorney fees were given. Only after the sale of the land I was awarded $5,000 for attorney fees from my relatives.

I had my last attorney fight for a higher rate of interest. The interest rate of a low 6% was given, but my last attorney fought for 12% and ended with that. My credit card rates were 18% at the time I borrowed to pay my taxes to the town.

My Aunt Marjorie filed for a Petition to Partition in 1992 just prior to my entering in the 20-year period for my Adverse

Possession case, which started in 1972. Given another year the 20 years would have gone by and the time element was on the line for my relatives. Action was taken by my aunt with the assistance of her son Peter, who guided her with the petition on the land.

Cousin Peter died of a heart ailment prior to the trial and his mother, my aunt, sat back while Cousin John took over for the silent heirs of the land. There was no clear deed to the land and the 23 acres would be sold and divided up by the 10 heirs who each would receive 10% from the sale of the land.

The town sent me a foreclosure notice while I was in the midst of this legal merry-go-round. I contacted the State Representative and explained my legal dilemma to him. The treasurer was hot on my trail to discourage me, and told me on the phone "Not to come home now." I immediately sent all of my cashier's checks showing proof of over 50% of my taxes paid to the town. Whatever the State Representative did, worked in my favor not to foreclose. If I had not had such a friend as the State Representative, I am sure things would have gone much worse. This was another attempt with the developer working with the town officials to eliminate having to pay me what was awarded to me from the court.

After the foreclosure notice was sent, I gathered up $10,000 dollars and another $10,000 from my fiancé Fred and sent it to the treasurer to bring my late tax fees up to date. I never would have received any compensation for all the years of paying taxes, interest or 10% as an heir of the land in dispute. I was not about to lose out on what my father and I had already paid to the town, during all those years of disappointment and heartache.

Receiving news, the trial did not go my way, I decided to file for an appeal and it cost me $2,500. I was appalled at my second attorney's total incompetence. The appeal was a total disaster with my attorney, who barely spoke with me. I never received the brief given for the appeal from my attorney until I demanded it from him. My second attorney was terminated and I sought out my last attorney from the Mid Cape area.

When you have no confidence with your attorney, it is all over. Trust was hard to find with an attorney after a trial and an appeal gone bad. I prayed this new attorney would conduct himself with fairness, and fight for his client without any persuasion of any kind. At the very beginning fairness was there I thought, but at the end of the litigation, I just prayed for a quick ending.

The next episode was receiving a letter from my Cousin John with an offer to buy our family property of 23 acres for $180,000. This cousin took over my aunt's position to be in charge of her Petition to Partition the land. Since I was the only heir paying the property taxes I needed to agree with this low offer. Then the land would be sold and the money derived from the sale of the land would be distributed to the 10 heirs.

The funny fact was my cousin sent the offer to buy the land and he used the same lawyer I had for my father's probate. Now you know what I mean about living in a small community of everyone knowing each other. My immediate reaction was no. I am not going to go with this offer, when I knew the property was worth much more than that! I declined his offer right away. I was not ready for that to happen.

During that time, I did not know if Cousin John was working just for himself and trying to beat the developer out of the land or not. It did not matter which way it went the land would eventually be sold and divided up.

The stage had been set many years prior to all the litigation I sought. The time had come for me to finally let go. The showdown was held in my first attorney's office where I stole my legal papers back from the secretary. I was supposed to go along with the powers that be in the corrupt town.

The only thing left for me to do was to bring in the retired developer, who abutted our family land in this dispute. Remember the property was in a land lock status due to the developer's Special Permit. That meant no other developer would be able to attend this privy auction. In order for this to happen Mr. Bertowski needed to go in front of a judge to be allowed to make an offer on our family land being auctioned. The judge gave an approval for him to be present at this auction. Cousin John mentioned he made an offer on the land and needed to mortgage his house. The judge stated he did not care what my cousin did with his house. I wished I would have had an attorney like him to really fight for me. Mr. Bertowski told me later my third attorney did not fight hard enough for me. That was my whole problem I never had any attorney really on my side. Also, I lived in California and if I would have remained on the Cape all those years, things may have ruled in my favor!

In the end I did not win the land. The developer acquired the land in a back-room deal. The land had gone down in value when my cousin and the developer wanted to buy. A real estate commissioner was involved with the sale from the Petition to Partition.

An auction for the land was set up in the attorney's office that represented the developer. This developer was the man who had a Special Permit on the land years ago and now I made his worst nightmare a reality. Mr. Bertowski had permission from the judge to make an offer on our family land now.

The law office was not far from the rotary on MacArthur Blvd. My Cousin John and his developer friend were present, along with the real estate commissioner. If I had any money of substance I would have attended and offered more than my cousin did. Paying my taxes for the land and attorney fees were all I could handle at that time.

My attorney and Mr. Bertowski were present and ready for the auction. Mr. Bertowski had no prior knowledge of the developer attending the auction along with my Cousin John. He believed it would be just my cousin John and himself.

They were all ready to make a sale on our old family woodlot; land that generation after generation of the seafaring Perry's had owned would be auctioned off. There was not a dam thing I could do about it. I was heart wrenched and waited helplessly to hear how the auction went.

The auction started at the low $180,000 and it went up while Mr. Bertowski bid higher as he watched Cousin John receive a sign from the developer to proceed higher with a nod of his head. That was their strategy my cousin doing the bidding with the developer's money to acquire this precious land. I could have been in that position like my cousin, and made the developer a much easier route to acquire the land he wanted for years. I made a decision long ago not to have any dealings with this man and I followed what was in my heart and soul. Other people would have jumped to be in the position like my cousin, but I have more blessings from God and possess a powerful gift from above. I have my peace of mind back, knowing I needed to go through this torment to be able to understand the blessings I possess now.

I received the call from Mr. Bertowski with the sad news he did not acquire the land. The bid ended at $260,000 and the developer won the land. Mr. Bertowski was mad and confronted my Cousin John's silent partner after the sale of the auction was finalized.It was as clear as a bell how corrupt they all were. Without Mr. Bertowski's attendance, I would not have the full knowledge of how my enemies operated against me to get what they wanted. Cousin Johnny did not have over $180,000, to acquire the land!

It appeared Cousin Johnny and the developer worked out a private deal of their own. At a later date I heard Johnny had some trouble with this developer and eventually did well for himself. I do know Cousin John was the only living relative who was as corrupt as the developer. Birds of a feather flock together.

After 20 years there are 3 acres on the old Perry land not sold yet, most likely due to the location being close to the wetlands. I heard Cousin John and the developer have incorporated now.

The money I received was not enough compensation for all the mental stress, forced savings on property taxes, attorneys not worthy of what I paid them and it goes on. Here is the breakdown I received for my share of the land after the auction. The total amount awarded to me was $74,000 from the land auction of $260,000. There were 10 heirs and received 10% each after the sale. I received all the property taxes including the interest for over 30 years and derived a 10% portion from the sale of the land. The sale from the land was only $10,000 and I was awarded $5,000 from my relatives for attorney fees they were required to pay me from the judge.

In all reality it was not worth it after paying attorney fees with 18% interest on all my credit cards including property taxes and trips to the Cape for legal matters. The irony with the rest of the relatives (included in the petition to partition) was they just sat back and collected the money I almost had a nervous breakdown over.

The true total was around $54,000 (Not deducting all attorney fees etc.) due to my late payment of $20,000 for late fees and penalties on my property taxes. This was necessary to avoid another foreclosure notice from the town. Fairness and trust had evaporated with that town.

Thanks to Mr. Bertowski the land jumped up $80,000 more for attending the land auction. It started at $180,000 and after the land auction went up to $260,000 I was grateful for that much and less profit for the developer to have. My last attorney stated to me a total of 9 houses could be built on the Perry woodlot of 23 acres due to several acres located in wetlands.

In the past years, the land had been rezoned from quarter acre lots to one acre lots and that meant less houses for the developer to be able to build. Larger homes would be built for one acre lots. It would cost around $200,000 to put roads and utilities in. I believe my attorney was trying to make me feel better of the overall added expenses to develop. At that time nothing made me feel better.

None of my relatives ever thanked me. I don't even think they really knew what was going on except for my Cousin John who attended the land auction. I never had a relationship with the relatives who were listed as heirs on the property and won't ever know what they thought of their unexpected inheritance. I assisted my relatives with extra money and I sure hope they spent their money wisely from our old family Perry woodlot.

I love all my brothers, but we all go our separate ways as many families do. Marriage gets involved and spouses are more connected with their immediate family and that's the way it is. Sometimes I think the harder you try to get along the worse it gets. So, you just let things go with family and allow life to take its course to sail without them. The love is there, but it is too difficult to express because of prior resentment, jealousy, pride and stubbornness. Life goes on without family and you pray for them to have good lives.

Hopefully later in life you may reconnect once more with love and forgiveness in your hearts. I never thought several brothers and I would drift apart like the ocean sands. We should have worked together despite our ill feelings or jealousy.

Now that I think about how my father left his share of the land to only me, excluding my brothers brought the awareness of the burden I needed to learn. If I had not taken on this long hardship to keep my promise to my father I may have lost my way. My faith was tested out of love for my biological father, the history and land of my ancestors and for the love for God. I found the true meaning of love in my past life meeting Jesus Christ himself. Being blessed to witness the words and love from Jesus has never left my soul.

I remained in California and found a house I really liked and paid the same amount the land was sold for, $260,000. My house has doubled in the last 20 years. The other interesting fact was I received my check from the sale of the land on Good Friday in 2001. My past life explains the spiritual connection for me on that special day.

I kept my promise to my father and ended up with a different type of richness. I lost the family land and in return, was granted a God-given miraculous gift of automatic writing through spirit in 1995 right after I lost my trial.

In my chapter A Narrow and Chilling Escape is given to show the importance of a past life experience. To understand your past can give your present life a new meaning of who you were and why you possess certain qualities now. After all was said and done, I knew there was a spiritual lesson of history connecting my soul. The love was there all along shining through from the past acknowledging my great faith.

Your past unfolds and with the great faith I acquired still continues on as I chose through my free will to study spiritualism for 10 years. This past life connected me to choose good over evil with an old enemy. I almost lost my life in the

Roman arena and was saved to go back to teach about Jesus to my people in Egypt. My present life the same enemy stole old family land and I am writing about Jesus through the blessings of writing through Spirit. My soul knew from the past not to trust this enemy and I was blessed to continue on a spiritual path of understanding my greatest past life. To be able to acquire this knowledge of connecting back to over two thousand years ago from a past life, has given me a new meaning as to why I went through this mental anguish.

I followed my free will when I cried to God to guide me to a church that would suit me. At that time, I did not know I would reconnect with past friends in this Spiritualist Church. They became my new family as I needed them in my life to teach me as I taught them in the past through Jesus.

I have reached a full circle with a spiritual journey of fulfillment due to my travels many years ago stumbling across the most important person. I thank God I carried this wisdom from long ago in my soul to not take the easy route with this past enemy. My faith was tested and I will enjoy writing with my new gift. It doesn't get any better than this!

EPILOGUE

On August 28, 2019, I asked who my spirit guide was, and the name Kurnack was given to me. I had always assumed my spirit guide was Isis, mother of all of Egypt. To my astonishment, I met Karnak, who gave me the correct spelling of his name; but told me his name was not important.

I respectfully agreed because of my desire to give him credit for being my friend and spirit guide during my journey. We both had a good laugh at this meeting of our souls.

Karnak said I am Egyptian and named after the Karnak Temple in Egypt. He had me circle like the temple on my paper ten times. This temple meant the most select of places. There was no doubt in my mind now of the spelling of his name. I definitely had my answer.

You were a powerful source, as we learned of the love of Jesus Christ for all people. I will be with you until you are done writing. You will finish your second book, and a third book will enter in, and you will give spiritual enlightenment to people.

You shall shine. I was there when you preached words of love from Jesus. I am only assisting you now to reconnect what you once taught. You were chosen to live and spread the words of Christ.

You will do it in book form and continue on with other spiritual endeavors. I was assigned to you to teach as you did in your past life. I am with you now and will remain to assist you along your travels. You are almost where you want to be, and your book will be published. You will take on a new meaning in life to become a spiritual author and teacher of spiritualism.

I asked: Why did it take so long for me to put my past life together? I am 66 years old, and will I have time to spread the words in my book? You will have another 20 years or more on earth. You will be heard through your writings and much more.

What was my name, if I was so well known in my village? Your first name was Assad, which means lion. You left your home and wife to travel to far-away areas to learn more. You are still the same, ALWAYS wanting more knowledge, and you did seek out the most extraordinary news ever! So much that you ended up in the arena and was almost killed there. You spoke loudly, and you will speak loud again in book form.

You are assisted now because you taught so many about Jesus Christ, and you will be looked up to again. You are a true story and a legend in your village. Not too many people did what you accomplished. Jesus loves you for spreading his words of love.

Now is the time for you to shine. It is coming, and your life will take on a new meaning of being able to serve Jesus again in book forms. I leave you, and when you need me, just ask for me.

Yes, indeed, I shall ask for you, as I finally have your name so I may ask for you! There is much more to come, and I am looking forward to working with my spirit guide Karnak.

Without the great love of God Almighty, Jesus, Karnak, and all the pure and highest forms of energy moving me on my spiritual journey, my book "Your Soul's History," would not have been created. Anything is possible with God!

ACKNOWLEDGEMENTS

First and foremost, I thank God for my rare gift of "automatic writing through spirit." Wisdom from above was bestowed upon me the ability to write like never before. I need to thank a friend from my past life and now in my present who chose to be with me as my Egyptian spirit guide. Karnak is his name and shares my journey, guiding me to explore more each and every day. It was his constant guidance, patience and love that carried me on year after year. I know he will be with me until the end of my journey here.

Thank you, Jacquie, for the huge green cross you gave me. I hung it on my wall as a daily reminder of my Divine healing during the darkest time in my life. It was my inspiration for my book cover!

Much love and appreciation to Reverend C.V. Mitchell, my mentor for ten years, studying spiritual understanding, meditation and healing classes at his chapel, Universal Christian Spiritualist Church. I was guided to his church and grew spiritually. This church became my new spiritual family during my darkest time. I thank Reverend Mitchell, Larry, Barbara and all the rest for their wisdom and love.

My love goes to my husband, Fred, always coming to my rescue with his computer knowledge and encouragement. Without his expertise, I would have been all over the place, as he kept me organized throughout my book. Fred edited my 90-minute regression, eliminating the long pauses to end up with an 18-minute uninterrupted regression.

Many thanks go to Connie Smith and her sister Jacquie Beveridge, for sending their family and friends for spiritual readings. They kept my gift flowing for those in need of spiritual nourishment.

I thank my friends, Anita Montgomery, Ginger Crosbie, Jacquie Beveridge, Barbara Marker and Sue Daly, for all their gifts of love when I really needed them during my spiritual journey. Friends are like treasures in the sand.

Most of all, I thank Louise Munro Foley for editing my book, giving me all the information on how to set up a manuscript and much more! Lou was a true blessing guiding me through each hoop I needed to jump through. She was my earth angel.

It was an honor to have met Peter Woodbury, who works with Edgar Cayce's Association for Research and Enlightenment. I attended a group hypnotic regression workshop with Peter, and the next day, I had the privilege to experience a private 90-minute regression. This past life regression intertwines perfectly with my present life. I deeply appreciate Peter for providing the truth of my most important past life, which has been etched in my soul forever.

I was blessed with my father and mothers constant love on earth and from the other side. To be able to communicate with them keeps me energized.

Made in the USA
Las Vegas, NV
31 August 2022

54404815R00094